Dating
Sucks

What to Do When Your
Love Life Makes You Miserable

Joanne Kimes

author of *Pregnancy Sucks*

Adams Media

New York London Toronto Sydney New Delhi

Adams Media
An Imprint of Simon & Schuster, Inc.
57 Littlefield Street
Avon, Massachusetts 02322

For information about special discounts for bulk purchases, please
contact Simon & Schuster Special Sales at 1-866-506-1949 or business@
simonandschuster.com.

The Simon & Schuster Speakers Bureau can bring authors to your live
event. For more information or to book an event contact the Simon &
Schuster Speakers Bureau at 1-866-248-3049 or visit our website at www.
simonspeakers.com.

Manufactured in the United States of America

Library of Congress Cataloging-in-Publication Data
Kimes, Joanne.
Dating sucks / Joanne Kimes.
p.   cm.
ISBN 1-59337-401-1
1. Dating (Social customs) 2. Man-woman relationships.
3. Mate selection. I. Title.
HQ801.K53 2005
306.73—dc22
2005005215

ISBN 978-1-59337-401-3

To my grandma Sally,
who gives the best back scratches in the whole world!

I love you.

contents

acknowledgments

At the risk of sounding like I just won an Oscar, I'd like to thank the following people:

I begin with the fine folks at Adams Media, without whom the book would never have been written. Well, I still would have written it, but it'd just be a thick stack of papers on my desk instead of something that's sold at a bookstore. I especially want to thank Gary M. Krebs and Kate Epstein, who both saw the need for a cathartic look at love. And also dear little Rifka, Kate's beautiful new daughter, who kept Kate so busy that I didn't have to write a formal proposal.

A big thank you to my agent, Jeff Herman who took me on as a client when no one else would. He's proven himself to be quite the savvy businessman, as well as a heck of a nice guy.

I also want to thank sensational singles like Meridith Weiss, Alexis Miller, Sheila Lawrence, Michele Raven, Lisa Caitin, Alexis White, Christy McBrayer, Claudia Ehrlich, Susanna Schick, Kathleen Laccinole, Michelle Havich, Eileen Aghekian, Nancy Bistritz, and Rabbi Rosen, who all generously shared their tales of dating woe with me.

A big thanks to the litany of losers that I went out with over the years for being so gross, strange, and just plain creepy. Although dating them was a truly retched experience, it did provide me with ample fodder to write this book.

Thank you Marjorie and Jim Praytor for having sex six years ago and creating Carlin, my daughter's best friend. If it wasn't for our kids' almost daily play dates during summer vacation, I would have never made my deadline.

(Uh oh, the red light is flashing and the orchestra's starting to play! Better sum this up!)

And last but *definitely* not least, thank you to my husband, Jeff, and my daughter, Emily. Not because they made this book any better, but because they made my life so much better. I love you both with all of my heart.

(The audience gives me a standing ovation and I'm escorted offstage by Brad Pitt. What? A girl can dream, can't she?)

introduction

I don't want to mislead anyone, so let me put my cards on the table right from the start. I'm married. I've been married to a wonderful man for seven years now. We have a beautiful daughter, a lazy dog that acts more like a houseplant, and a stubborn trail of ants that I can't seem to get rid of no matter what I do. But just because I've promised to love, honor, and pick up my husband's dirty underwear off the bathroom floor till death do us part, does not mean that I got to this point easily. In fact, as you're well aware, finding a man who you want to share the rest of your life with is like finding a piece of hay in a needle stack. You know it's there, but to find it you'll have to go through a lot of little pricks.

So why, you may ask, is a married woman writing a book about the perils of dating? That's a very valid question. For one thing, I have a great deal of experience in the dating milieu. In fact, I like to think of myself as an M.D., a master dater. I had my first date in the seventh grade when Michael Kratchman asked me if I wanted to hang out with him at the All-American Burger after school, and my last date at the age of thirty-five when my then-boyfriend got down on one knee and asked me to marry him. So when you do the math, I've had a total of twenty-three years of on the job training. If dating only had a 401K program, I'd be set for life!

Also, it's not as if I dated only one man for all those years. I've dabbled in every species of man from the smart ones to the dumb ones, and the cute ones to the not so cute ones. I've gone out with ones that smothered me and ones that couldn't commit. I've dated men who put me on a pedestal and others who put my heart through a paper shredder. I've been through more men than the U.S. Marines.

And finally, not to toot my own horn, but I'm pretty much an expert when it comes to complaining. In fact, I've written two books that focus on how unfair life can be, *Pregnancy Sucks* and *Pregnancy Sucks for Men*. When you think about it, dating is a great way to prepare yourself for pregnancy. In both instances you have to endure months of pain and awkwardness in order to achieve a wonderful goal. With pregnancy, you have to battle gas, constipation, and hemorrhoids. With dating, you face rejection, low self-esteem, and hours waiting by the phone. And, in both cases, after all your suffering, you end up sharing your life with a gassy, whiny, demanding baby.

The process of dating encapsulates so many horrific aspects to it that bookstores have devoted shelf upon shelf to the process. The titles assure you that the how-to's of dating are as easy as planting a garden. Problem is, with dating there are a lot more bad seeds to sow before the flowers bloom. Most books out there deal with tricks and games on how to find him, how to keep him, and how to get him on one knee within six months.

So what, pray tell, does this book promise? Absolutely nothing. If you buy this book, I promise you zilch. No husband. No fiancé. Not even a guy who'll drive you to the airport. Nothing, that is, but compassion, a good perspective, and a much-needed shoulder to cry on. . . . Well, not an actual shoulder really—more like an absorbent page to dry away your tears on your journey for love. And, if you do find a wonderful loving man to be with, promise me one thing: If you can ever figure out how to get him to pick up his own dirty underwear, please let me know how you did it. Thanks!

why go out when there's so much good stuff on tv?

It's true. Dating sucks. It sucks big time. Chances are if you've been dating for any length of time, you've experienced the rejection, heartache, and utter disgust that the entire dating process can bring. You hate the stupid rules and playing the silly games, and you long for the days of yesteryear when the world was a simple place and arranged marriages were all the rage.

Back then finding a husband was a no-brainer. As soon as your parents cutteth your cordeth, they betrothed you to the baby boy down the cobblestone street. Of course, they had to sweeten the deal by throwing in five healthy chickens and a bushel of nice beets, but after that, the deal was set. As soon as you reached the advanced age of fourteen, you and your acne-ridden fiancé were married in a ceremony that forbade dancing, drinking, and merriment of any kind. You had your sixth child before you left your teen years, and died at the ripe old age of twenty-seven from a toenail infection that went horribly awry.

1

But those were the good old days, and today the burden of finding a soul mate is yours and yours alone. Because of this, you wander through the dating meat market in search of a nice bull and pray that you don't choose one with mad cow disease. As if this scenario isn't bad enough, you're forced to compete with millions of other heifers with their fancy ear tags, who jiggle around to show off their new silicone utters.

You know from experience that finding your Mr. Right is going to be difficult. Out of the thousands of men that you see each year while at work, running errands, and going about your day, there may be only a handful of them that make your heart pound any faster. Since most of them are either gay or married or makes a gross noise when they chew, you give your heart and your body to the only remaining one. In return, this loser lies or cheats or does any number of things that make you eat your weight in chocolate. And even if a miracle does happen and you find someone to love and cherish till death do you part, your chances of ever reaching your aluminum anniversary are just under 50 percent.

So why do we go through this futile search to find love at all? Why aren't we just content to stay home every night, sitting on our overstuffed sofas and watching all those great shows on TV? After all, with satellite television there are hundreds of channels at our disposal, so there's always something good on, even when it's something bad. What makes us reach for the remote and click off *E! True Hollywood Story* and get back in the dating game once again? Why, oh why do we voluntarily put ourselves through the pain, humiliation, and suffering that dating can inflict on us time and time again?

The truth is that there is more than just one answer to these questions. In fact, there are several of them to choose from, which is quite helpful to me since I'm devoting this entire first chapter to the subject and would hate for it to be only a page or two long.

So let's do it, shall we? Let's explore some of the most common reasons to put on our tankinis and dive back into the dating pool once again.

Pressure from Your Friends

Peer pressure can be a powerful thing. It's what made you take your first hit off a cigarette and buy those trendy crop pants, even though they made you look like an Oompa Loopma. Peer pressure is also another big reason why you decide to go out when all you really want to do on a Saturday night is stay home and try out those sticky things that pull off the blackheads from your nose.

Your once-single friends who are in deep, committed relationships are the worst. Instead of talking about the latest movie or the newest diet trend, all they do is ramble on and on about how great it is to have a boyfriend. They tell you that they've never been happier or more fulfilled and that they want to help you find your way down this path of enlightenment. It seems that your formerly single friends are now like Relationship Jehovah's Witnesses, and you have suddenly become their airport.

These born-again friends are constantly trying to fix you up with guys who are suddenly single. Now that your friends are in the loop of love, they're somehow privy to insider dater trading. They know which couples are having trouble and who's breaking up with whom. Because of these hot tips, they can now set you up with guys who are back on the dating market before another buyer scoops them up.

If you say no to these fix-ups, your friends will become more devious in their attempts to show you the way. They'll invite you out to dinner, and since you already tried that blackhead-removal thing, which worked beautifully I might add, you tag along. But at some point after you place your drink order and before the bread basket arrives, a "friend" will suddenly come up to your table. Surprise! You've been fixed up after all. These cult members are really quite tricky!

You may still have a few single girlfriends that linger about, but one by one, they're dropping off like flies. And in some cases, when "once-single friend" becomes part of a couple, you can feel a dramatic shift in your relationship. You no longer spend Saturday nights together if neither of you have a date. She cancels plans with you at the last minute because "he" finally calls. And suddenly she's having dinner parties for couples only, as if setting an odd amount of plates somehow throws off the time-space continuum. It seems that once your "she" becomes a "we," you can kiss that friendship *buh-bye*.

Sure, you want to be part of their brave new world. You too want to be part of a "we." Although it may be depressing, this peer pressure may be just the motivation you need to push yourself back out into the dating world once again. But take my advice: When you go out there, do yourself a favor and leave those crop pants at home.

The real reasons why your friend who is in a relationship is trying to pair you off:

- She doesn't want to worry that her boyfriend will dump her for her available friends.
- She thinks that double-dating is so "cute."
- She hates her boyfriend's friends and she hopes you'll go out with someone better that he can hang out with.

- She wants someone to bitch with about the stresses of making the relationship work. Misery does love company, you know.
- She wants you to buy new date clothes that she can borrow.

Pressure to Find the Last Good Guy Out There Before Someone Else Grabs Him

There are many different reasons why it can be so hard to find a man. Maybe you've been hurt before and it's hard to give your heart away again. Maybe it's because you don't love yourself enough to let someone else love you back. Or maybe it's because, when it comes right down to it, most men are just butt ugly.

I myself am a firm believer in this theory. Sure, there are a few guys out there that are the exception to this rule, like George Clooney, Brad Pitt, and Matthew Broderick (maybe it's just me, but I think he's precious). These stud muffins make our heart go pitter-patter and give us the confidence we need to assure ourselves that, despite some confusing thoughts back in junior high, we are indeed heterosexual. But when you take the group as a whole, most men are about as appealing as stone-washed jeans.

This trait of having one sex that's more attractive than the other is nothing new. Most every other animal species displays some sort of favoritism when it comes to having better looks. With peacocks for instance, it's the males that are the more attractive of the species with their brilliantly colored tail feathers. With lions, the males dominate as well with their thick golden manes. But when it comes to human beings, it's the men who are seen as second-rate because of their thinning hair, paunchy physique, and external genitalia.

This fact is no secret to us women. We've known for eons that we'll never find a man who is more attractive then we are, so we've chosen to focus our interests on other traits, like kindness and a sense of humor, which are more important than a powerful jaw line. Because the selection of attractive men is so slim, we've had to strengthen our desire for other qualities, not unlike a blind man who's developed a stronger sense of smell.

When you think about it, you know I'm right. How often have you spotted a good-looking woman with an unattractive man and thought nothing of it? But if you ever see an attractive man with an unattractive woman, you stop dead in your tracks and assume that the only reason he's with her is because she has the unique ability to swallow a kielbasa whole.

Even with our evolved understanding of men, the lack of selection is still a big problem. We know that if we take the millions of single men out there and subtract the ones that are married, involved in a serious relationship, haven't committed a heinous crime, aren't freeloaders, winos, or cheats, and don't want to dress up in women's clothing, we're left with only a handful of good men. This, of course, fills you with the intense pressure to find one of them before another woman beats you to it. Face it, girls: When it comes to finding a good guy, the pickings are so slim that we fight over them as if they were the last diet Coke at a picnic.

Pressure from the Competition

Although there are some great things about living in this modern age, like caller ID and the invention of the shelf bra, there are some disadvantages to it as well. Little Half-Pint didn't know how easy she had it back on the prairie. Whenever Manley asked her out, all she had to do to get ready was pinch her cheeks and remove any stray vermin that had nested in her hair. Back then women weren't obsessed with having shiny hair and lips that were plumped up by their own ass fat.

But today, the competition's fiercer than ever before because there are millions of other competitors who are after the same prize that you are. Because of this you need help from the experts before going into the ring with the women with 6 percent body fat and bellybutton rings. You need a hairdresser for highlights every six to eight weeks. You need a dentist to bleach your teeth as white as liquid paper. You need a tanning salon for sun-kissed skin and a manicurist for weekly fills. And, of course, you need a personal trainer to give you abs of steel and a plastic surgeon to give you breasts like them.

Before some women put up their dating dukes, they get the help that only a by-product of the botulism bacteria can provide. Yes, they step into their dermatologist's office for a regular injection of Botox to paralyze their facial muscles. One of the most prominent dermatologists is Dr. Peter Goldman. He has an office in the Beverly Hills area and has examined more stars than the Hubble telescope. He estimates that 25 percent of his Botox clientele are single women under the age of forty. And even more surprising is that many of these clients are actually even in their twenties. I can't begin to fathom why anyone so young would want a face that lacks expression—they can't all be professional poker players.

All of the work we have to do to keep ourselves in the game is expensive and exhausting, and we wonder why we can't find love by just being ourselves. Why can't we stroll through the dating scene without curled eyelashes and dewy cheeks? But then at the next party or social gathering you go to, the reason hits you like a Long Island Iced Tea. Here's how it goes down:

1. You spot a cute guy from across the room.
2. You make eye contact with him and he smiles.
3. He heads your way, and your mind races with the possibilities! Is he the one? Is this the moment I'll recount to our future children?
4. In an instant your fantasy comes to a screeching halt when he makes a beeline for the D-cup standing right behind you.
5. You head toward the food table for that handful of M&Ms you've managed to resist up until now.

Face it. It's a jungle out there and our competition is fiercer than ever before. Because of this we have to go to extremes to keep up with the young, flawless Joneses. Or do we? Do we really have to spend the rest of our lives draining our bank accounts and risking our health in order to retain our youth? The way I see it, plastic surgery is like amassing nuclear weapons. We just keep attaining more and more of it simply to keep up with the competition. If everyone gets breast implants, then we have to get breast implants *and* a brow lift to keep up. Can't we stop the madness before we have so many face-lifts that we have to breastfeed from our necks? If we can simply agree to stop outdoing each other with both plastic surgery and weapons of mass destruction, the world would be a better place despite a few brow lines and crow's-feet.

The sad part of it all is that women are spending about $6,000 to get those trendy, gravity-defying implants that may soon be out of fashion. These hooter-impaired women don't realize that only a generation ago the desirable fashion look was to have a small chest. A figure like a minute hand was much more sought after than that of an hourglass.

In order to keep up with ever-changing fashion trends and to save a fortune in plastic surgery alterations, I propose that they make breast implants similar to Air Jordan shoes. That way, women could easily pump their breasts up or down to coincide with their desired look.

Fortunately there are plenty of self-confident women out there who don't feel like they need to cut open their body and fill it with something that will outlive them by 400 years in order to attract a man. Not only do these healthy women have a great body image, but, the way I see it, they also have an extra six grand to play around with. If you're one of those confident women, here are some suggestions on how you can spend your newfound cash that will attract the opposite sex with the same magnitude:

1. Open up a KC Masterpiece franchise in your backyard.
2. Get season tickets to your city's football team.
3. Buy the best home theater on the market with the biggest plasma screen and give him total control of the remote.
4. Turn your guest room into a beer distillery.
5. Buy $6,000 worth of power tools.
6. Replumb your house so that chocolate milk flows from the tap.
7. Have a muralist paint a life-size picture of Pamela Anderson on your bedroom ceiling.

8. Bribe the head honcho at KFC to find out what their eleven herbs and spices are and incorporate them in all of your cooking.
9. Hire Jack Nicklaus to come over and teach your dates how to improve their swing.
10. Put up a deer stand in your front yard and use the rest of the dough to buy a closet full of kick-ass shoes.

Pressure from Your Family

Show me a single woman who doesn't feel pressure from her parents to get married and I'll show you a single woman who's an orphan. It seems to me that being the parents of a grown child somehow entitles these parents to certain privileges. They can criticize that child in every way, they can show every visitor their child's naked baby pictures, and they can ask their child over and over again the inevitable gut-wrenching question, "So, when are you going to settle down and give us grandchildren?"

The whole idea of parents pushing you into procreating always strikes me as funny. Back in high school, the main reason that your parents' existed was to keep you forever a virgin. You had to abide by their long list of rules when it came to boys or else pay the price of being forbidden to use Sun-In for an entire month. You were not allowed to have a boy in your room unless you left the door open. You couldn't stay out past nine o'clock on the weekends. And you couldn't go over to a boy's house unless his parents and certain representatives of the armed forces were going to be there as well.

But now all that has changed. These days your folks encourage you to go out with any guy you please as long as he doesn't have a criminal record or hasn't sustained an injury that's left him sterile. If they'd have known earlier on that you would remain childless for so many years, they would have never given you that awkward birds and bees talk that left you with so many disturbing visuals. Sure, you may have gotten knocked-up as a teenager, but at least your parents would have been able to see their grandchildren before they were too old to pick them up.

This familial pressure isn't restricted to your mother and father. It seems that every member of your family tree has an opinion about your state of nonmatrimony and it makes you want to take an ax to each and every last branch. Uncle Fred warns you that if you keep being so picky, you're destined to become an old maid. Aunt Myrtle sends you dating articles from *Cosmo* that she clipped out while having her hair dyed blue. Even your grandma advises that you should never have broken things off with your fiancé, even though you found him in bed with your best friend. Sure, he may have cheated from time to time, but at least you could say that you were married.

Because of their constant abuse, you now dread going to family functions. Every member of your gene pool makes you feel like you're going to drown. They have the power to make you feel insignificant simply because you don't have a significant other. As you sit there at the kiddie table along with your other single relatives, most of who are still in diapers, you listen in on the adult conversation. You hear about the latest neighbor to get married or the one who just found out that she's pregnant. At some point you chime in about how your medical staff is close to finding the cure for cancer, but this trivial tidbit is overshadowed by the enchanting tale of how little Janie found her mother's diaphragm and used it as a hat for her dolly.

Married siblings can be a huge source of pressure to start dating again. Suddenly the brothers and sisters that you would let practice making hickeys on your arm are not on the same level as you anymore. For some reason, when they say "I do" your parents instantly view them as grownups, while you remain someone who still needs help cutting your meat. This situation becomes even more catastrophic if you have a younger sibling who's getting married. As she walks down the aisle, no one seems to look at the beautiful bride. Instead they all stare at you as if waiting for your mental breakdown to set in. You want to shout out to everyone, "It's okay! I'm really happy for her. I promise!" But what you're really thinking is "Pass me the wedding cake, NOW, God damn it!"

Yes, when it comes to feeling pressure to get back onto the playing field of love, your family can be one big, giant pressure cooker. To release some of the steam, I suggest that you do the following:

- Give your parents photographs of your friend's children. When it comes right down to it, all your parents really want are pictures to show off to their friends. If you think they really want to spend their

66 Whenever my family gets together, they all seem to pity me because I'm not married. They put on these sad faces like there's something wrong with me. It's too bad the government doesn't view us single women the way that our families do, because we'd get a handicapped parking permit out of the deal. 99

—Rebecca

time cleaning projectile vomit and poopy diapers, you're crazy.

- When one of your family members says something biting, bite them back. If your aunt tells you that you're being too picky, tell her that she would have benefited from this strategy and wouldn't have to spend her life married to a loser who gambled away their nest egg.
- Light a scented candle at the kiddie table. It will mask some of the odors and make it a much sweeter-smelling place to sit.

Pressure from Society

Just when you thought that you couldn't handle any more pressure, society adds its own two cents worth. It pushes you into dating because it forces upon you the notion that it's so darn miserable to live alone. Everywhere you turn, society rubs your state of singleness in your face. You can't flip through a magazine without seeing a pair of happy air-brushed lovers in an embrace. You can't stand in a movie line without being mocked by some pimply teenage couple in front of you holding hands. Hell, you can't even drive in the carpool lane no matter how congested the freeway is simply because you don't have a man to call your own. It's heartless the way our culture will protest the use of animal testing, but has no qualms about making singles feel as if they were the last ones picked for lover's dodge ball.

If you don't have a significant other, you can't even enjoy the simple pleasures that life has to offer, like going out for a romantic meal. When you go to a restaurant solo, they stick you at a table near the kitchen, you're denied any two-for-one specials, and are shunned from ordering certain dishes like a Caesar salad simply because they only make them for two. Worse still are the other patrons who stare at you in pity as if you were some sick dog forced to wear one of those funnel collars.

Even harder to endure are the national holidays that society has created. Sure, they tell us that they commemorate some special event, but deep down you know that the only reason they exist is so that big business can make a killing from torturing you. The following are some of the hardest days on the calendar for a single girl, each of which may just give you the incentive you need to go back out in the dating world:

Valentine's Day: Single women all over the country fear this day like a cold speculum. We know that as we sit home alone stuffing our faces with bon-bons from self-purchased heart-shaped boxes of candy, millions of happy couples are enjoying themselves and exchanging bodily fluids.

Christmas: The yuletide season is another big hurdle to get over. There's something about a winter wonderland and good will toward man that makes us want to shoot ourselves in the head. We know that because of the lack of a better, more handsome option, we'll be forced to spend yet another holiday season at our parents' house. The only way that we can make love in front of a roaring fire would involve taking matters into our own hands and a mental image of Colin Ferrell. Oh, how we long to spend the holidays sipping warm eggnog with a man that we love so much, that we don't even care we're at risk of contracting salmonella with every sip we take.

Birthdays: Once we get past the age of parties that include piñatas and patent leather shoes, the only thing that we really want on our birthday is to get laid. As we blow out an ever-growing number of candles, fire extinguisher in hand, we make the same wish that we do every year: that this will finally be the year that we find love.

New Year's Eve: This is the most pressure-filled holiday of them all. As the end of each year approaches, we single women scurry around for dates like paparazzi on Britney Spears. We know that if we don't have someone to kiss on the stroke of midnight, our Fairy Godmother will give up all hope of us ever finding our prince and will move on to a more worthy cause, like Greenpeace.

Mother's Day: Don't even get me started! Year after year we've been buying our mom thoughtful little trinkets without getting anything in return. When will it be our turn to have someone make us a macaroni necklace and a handmade card? When will we be served burnt toast in bed by our own freckle-faced cherubs who grow up to be ungrateful and demanding and only call us when they need money?

If this nation truly believes in equality no matter one's race, creed, or religion, it should balance out the holidays with some that pay tribute to the American Single Woman. I propose that Congress enact holidays that celebrate the lives of some of the saints of singledome in order to balance out the ones that cause such holiday injustice:

Mary Tyler Moore Day: If there's one woman who's made single-living acceptable, it's the woman who could turn the world on with her smile. She along with her wacky sidekick Rhoda Morgenstern took the *sin* out of "sin-gle."

Dolley Madison Day: Sure she was the most beloved first lady of the century, but more importantly, she inspired a whole line of tasty baked goods that provide comfort to millions of single women.

Meg Ryan Day: Where would we singles be without *Sleepless in Seattle, You've Got Mail,* and the quintessential favorite, *When Harry Met Sally.* Women across the country still find fellow-feeling in words like, "It's not that he didn't want to get married, it's that he didn't want to marry me."

Whoever Invented the AA Battery Day: These underappreciated objects are crucial in providing power to favorites of single women everywhere like the Pocket Rocket and the Bunny. I can't think of any other one person throughout history that has brought more satisfaction to single women.

That Girl Day: This holiday would pay tribute to that cute and inspiring character played by Marlo Thomas. Yes, I know technically she wasn't really single in the show since she dated good ol' Donald Hollinger, but she was so dang adorable that there really should be a day that celebrates her anyway.

Pressure from Mother Nature

Although Mother Nature can be a lovely gal who supplies us with springtime flowers and babbling brooks, she can also be quite a pushy broad. Every month she gives us horrible cramps as if she's screaming that we'd better have a child soon, before time—and our egg supply—runs out. We

" At least once a month my mother would send me a clipping from a magazine article that discussed the decline of fertility as a woman ages. It used to make me really mad until I decided to send my own articles, like the horrid state of nursing homes today. I think she got the message because now she only sends me cash."

—Melissa

know from our days back in Junior High health class that women are born with only a finite amount of these plump, juicy devils and if we wait too long to have them fertilized, they'll shrivel up like little ovarian raisins.

In decades past, women thought that they had years to reproduce. We erroneously believed that our bodies could conceive and carry a baby well into our forties. So what if we were so old that we would need a walker before our kid did. What was really important was that we had a long and fulfilling career, as well as a beefy investment portfolio.

But now recent studies tell us that it was all one big fat lie. Today's findings suggest that fertility starts to decline while we're still in our thirties, sometimes even earlier.

What's even more unfair is that this type of reproductive pressure is reserved solely for us women. Unlike the finite amount of eggs that women are born with, men produce millions of sperm every day while at work or at play (and we thought we women were great multitaskers!). True, their fertility does decrease with age as well, but as we know, it takes only one of those little buggers to make its way to the egg. Because of this difference, men don't feel the same intense pressure to settle down and start a family. They don't

have an internal biological clock that ticks with the magnitude of Big Ben. Instead, they have a sperm factory that
turns out more goods than an overseas sweatshop.

Even though the facts may sound depressing, I've lived
long enough to know one thing for certain: no one knows a
damned thing. As a teen I gave up my beloved French fries
because doctors told me they cause acne. Now that's been
disproved. I gave up drinking milk if I had a cold because
experts said it creates mucus. Now they tell us it doesn't.
Sure, they're saying that it's harder to conceive when you're
older, but mark my words, one day we'll be laughing at this
"fact" as well. Besides, if it's so impossible for women over
forty to conceive, why are they the second highest group of
women who experience unwanted pregnancies? See, I told
you. No one knows a damned thing.

Besides, even if some women will have a difficult time con-
ceiving when they're older, that doesn't mean that you have to
be one of them. By the time you're ready to start a family, science will no doubt have progressed to the point where getting
pregnant will be as easy as getting a pap smear. Just one long
Q-tip and two stirrups later, voilà, you're knocked up.

What good does it do to worry about this stuff anyway?
It's not going to change a thing. Does worrying about the
depleting rain forest grow any more trees? Does stressing
out about the demise of a *Sex and the City* movie make Sarah
Jessica Parker and Kim Cattrall get along any better? No.
And neither does worrying about the quality of your future
reproductive cycle. Instead, focus on more productive and
fulfilling goals that will give your life more enjoyment, like
starting a letter-writing campaign begging those two fine
actresses to reunite and make that damn movie already, for
heaven's sake!

Pressure from Father Time

There's someone else in cahoots with Mother Nature, which makes finding a soul mate even that much more of a challenge. That force is Father Time. Every year he drains us of our youth faster than a Jacuzzi is drained after some kid has pooped in it. We examine ourselves in our magnifying mirrors to see how much sap he's sucked from our tree. As the hands of Father Time tick away, we no longer have the energy that we used to have to stay out all night, or the metabolism to eat junk food without getting fat.

As we age we take on a more desperate attitude toward dating as well. It's now become a game of romantic musical chairs and we don't want to be the last one standing while other girls sit on the laps of the cute eligible men. We realize that we can't waste any time dating guys who aren't marriage material the way we used to do when we were younger. We're aware that as we get older there are less fish in the sea who want to go out with us, because they prefer to date guppies.

When we were young, we felt immortal. We didn't care about the repercussions of baking in the sun all day with strong tea mixed with baby oil rubbed onto our skin. We thought that when we grew older we'd embrace our wrinkles and not get caught up in trivial things like crow's-feet and frown lines. But now we struggle to regain our youthful appearance by buying expensive creams that contain everything from fruit acid to sheep placenta. We find ourselves fascinated by shows like *Extreme Makeover,* and we pull back our skin in front of the mirror to see what we'd look like with an eye job or face-lift (come on, I know you've done it).

Why do we obsess about staying young and beautiful? I'll tell you exactly why. It's because of the stupid men who obsess about women that are young and beautiful. Why can't they realize that beauty is only skin-deep and that it's what's on the inside that's truly important? Men don't seem all that concerned with what's on the inside as long as it's wrapped up in the skin of a woman who looks like a super-model. Their obsession with this rare breed is as much of a mystery to me as the success of Whoopi Goldberg.

To complicate the matter even further, women have this pressure to be married by the time they reach thirty. I imagine that this "rule" was set up many, many generations ago when the lifespan of humans was drastically shorter than it is now. If a woman didn't procreate early she wouldn't be around to see her grandkids. Also, since people died so young, staying married wasn't much of a problem. But now, thanks to the invention of antibiotics and good facial cream, women are living longer and looking better than ever. Therefore, I think that once the government finds a solution for the nation's health care crisis, it should focus on updating this "marry by the time you reach thirty" injustice.

Besides, if a woman marries young, she stands a far greater chance of her marriage ending in divorce. Again, when people died much earlier, being married for life wasn't much of a problem. Marriages ending in divorce were unheard of but those that ended in disease, draught, or infection were all the rage. Back then women never had to put up with the stresses of today's marriage: raising a family with both parents working, decades of monogamy, and the constant fighting over the setting of the thermostat.

In sum, relax. Try not to give in to today's pressure to stay forever young so that if we don't get married early like we're supposed to, at least we can look the part. As Bob

Dylan said, "The times, they are a-changin'," and it's about time that Father Time changed right along with them.

Pressure from Yourself

Of all the pressures to be in a relationship, one of the strongest is that which you inflict upon yourself. If you're a confident, independent woman, or just someone who's grown up watching Oprah, you know that life has meaning even without a significant other to call your own. You know that you don't need a man to feel complete and that you can live a happy and productive life with your friends, your family, and your TiVo.

But once in a while, your belief system comes to a crashing halt. Maybe it's when you get a wedding invitation that's addressed to you and a guest, and you realize that you don't have a guest to invite. Or maybe it's when you buy a DVD player and can't figure out how to get that damned thing to stop flashing 12:00. Or it could be when you get a terrible itch in the middle of your back that you can't for the life of you seem to reach.

It's at these moments that you're hit with loneliness that cuts you deeper than your thong underwear. No single woman that has ever walked on the face of this planet has been completely spared from loneliness. It doesn't matter if her family life was like that of the Waltons or that of the Mansons. It doesn't matter if she's a minimum-wage worker employed at McDonald's or a business executive working for The Donald. Loneliness is an equal opportunity annoyer and no one is spared from its wake.

Feeling lonely isn't the only thing that motivates you to get back out in the dating world once again. Maybe you're getting bored with being alone. Maybe your ex is getting married for the second time. Or maybe it's because you got yet another request to be a bridesmaid for a friend who's moving over to the dark side. Suddenly it's as if everyone else in the world has a partner but you. Everyone else has a sex life but you. And while we're at it, everyone else but you seems to find those really great parking spots right in front of the mall entrance.

The Best Things about Being Single

By all means, when the pressure of being single get to be too much, go back into the suckiness of dating. But until that time, remember that there are some great things about not having a man in your life:

1. You don't have to wear thong underwear.
2. You can wear a facial mask any night you want.
3. You don't have to deal with birth control.
4. You don't have to hold in your farts.
5. The underwear you find on the bathroom floor is your own.
6. You can chew your food with your mouth open.
7. You can belt out a Donna Summer song with a spoon for a microphone anytime you want.
8. You don't have to give a crap about your bikini line.
9. You don't have to go to anyone else's company parties.
10. You control the remote at all times.

chapter two

the directory of duds

Now that the pressure has built up enough for steam to come out of your ears, it's time to cool down by plunging into the dating pool. But before you take off those cute little flip-flops with the kitty cat heel and dive right in, I want to enlighten you as to what kinds of fish you're going to find splashing around with you. I know how hard it can be to get back into that icy water once you've been out of it for so long. Some women, the ones whose chest can double as a floatation devise, have no problem jumping back in. Others have to go in toe by toe, slowing down even more when they get to the sensitive areas. I know how hard it is to find a wonderful, loving man to share the rest of your life with. It's hard just to find a so-so guy who won't steal your wallet when you're out of the room. I know; I speak from experience. And I know I'm not alone.

Take my friends for instance. It always amazes me when one of them introduces me to one of her new loves. It's obvious from the first moment that I see them together how positively wrong he is for her. He's either too boring or

23

self-centered or any one of a million things that can go wrong with a man. It's apparent to everyone around her that this guy is not good enough for her. Everyone that is, except her.

The reason this astounds me so much is that I've gone shopping with these women. I've seen one of my friends painstakingly search dozens of stores to find the perfect white T-shirt in the exact blend of cotton and desired thickness. If she ever finds such a T-shirt, she'll invariably find some hidden flaw that's only visible under a microscope. She'll then send the salesgirl to the back to find another one that's of museum quality. If this poor woman comes out empty-handed, she'll force her to call all the other chains across the globe in a desperate attempt to track one down as if she's conducting her own fashion Amber Alert.

But when it comes to picking a life mate, my friend suddenly becomes a shopaholic who will take anything that's thrown her way. She'll go out with any guy that shows the slightest bit of interest. A smile and a "hello" will get the guy a date, and a "You have nice eyes" will buy him a romp in the hay. I think that if women were as picky about men as they are about clothing, there'd be far fewer breakups.

My only explanation for this mystery is that women don't have a place they can go to do some comparison-shopping for men. When it comes to their wardrobe, there are malls to stroll through, magazines to browse, and Web sites to cybershop in search of the latest styles. But there doesn't seem to be any place a girl can turn to find out the different styles of men there are to choose from. That is until now. I've compiled a list of the most common types of pariahs that swim freely in the dating pool.

The Fixer-Upper

The concept behind the Fixer-Upper is a valid one. Rachel Ashwell, the creator of Shabby Chic, has cashed in on this idea for years. She'll find a broken-down chest of drawers, slap on a few coats of whitewash, screw in some decorative crystal drawer pulls, and sell it for the equivalent of a spa weekend at the Golden Door. Many visionaries have attempted to use this same system on men, but it doesn't always translate quite as well. They find what they think to be an old piece of coal and envision a shiny diamond after all their efforts. The problem is that more times than not, all they end up with is a chunk of cubic zirconia.

It's easy to get suckered in by a Fixer-Upper. You'll meet him and not take much notice. But he'll say or do something that makes you think that there's more to him under the surface. Maybe he tells you that he's a poet, or an artist, or that he has a villa in the south of France. Whatever the reason, this forgettable man will suddenly become unforgettable.

Example of a Fixer-Upper

Pig Pen from Peanuts. You can wash him and scour him until his skin is sore, but he'll still have that plume of dust that trails behind him like a small mushroom cloud.

So you take him on as your little weekend project. You strap on your tool belt and get down to work. You're like Ty Pennington and he's your extreme makeover. You strip off his moldy exterior and apply some pinstriped siding. You shape up his roofline with a Sassoon trim and styling gel, and soon he starts to shine. This once-dilapidated figure of a man is now transformed into one that's good-looking and strong, and the envy of the whole neighborhood. But as you spend time with your new creation, you'll notice that some cracks begin to appear. The walls start to settle and the floor begins to warp, and you realize that even with all of these new cosmetic changes, the foundation of your Fixer-Upper simply wasn't as strong as you had hoped.

You wonder if you did anything wrong. As it turns out, the only mistake that you made was thinking that you had a piece of coal to begin with. All you really had was a piece of crap, and as we all know, you can't polish a turd. So the next time that you meet a Fixer-Upper, save yourself a whole lot of time and trouble, and find a guy that's in "ready to move in" condition.

Mr. Cheapo

There are many undesirable traits that you can overlook in a man. A receding hairline. A soft belly. You can even learn to accept a love of porn, because—face it—if you didn't, there'd be no one left to date. But the one trait that I personally just can't seem to accept is cheapness. I think that this characteristic is downright ugly. There are actually two forms of cheapness to look out for. The first kind is a guy who simply can't afford to buy things. The second is one that can afford to buy things but chooses not to. The latter is the one that I have a problem with.

My first encounter with a Mr. Cheapo was right after I had my heart broken. I was at my neighbors drowning my sorrows in strawberry cheesecake, when her friend Rob popped by. He seemed interested in me and pumped up my sagging ego like a miracle bra. He met my basic requirements in a man by telling me that I was cute and laughing at all of my jokes. So I decided to reward him by accepting his offer to take me out.

We went to a casual restaurant and had a good time, but when the check arrived, he only put down his share of the money. My inner voice told me to end it right there, but I figured that I'd give him another chance, given how hard it was to find a guy who met even my minimum basic requirements. For our second date, Rob took me to a flea market but only paid his own $5 admittance fee. It was then that I realized we were at the perfect location for me to dump this guy—among the other cheap junk.

Mr. Cheapos are easy to recognize from your very first date. You'll notice that when the waiter brings the check to your table, beads of sweat will form on Mr. Cheapo's forehead. He'll struggle to put his charge card down as if it were an infant he's leaving with a new sitter. If you decide to date a Mr. Cheapo, you can expect to celebrate your birthdays at Denny's because you'll get your meal for free. And most of your dates will consist of trips to the public museum, long strolls through the park, a day of shopping at the ninety-nine-cent store, and any restaurant that accepts coupons.

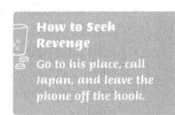

How to Seek Revenge
Go to his place, call Japan, and leave the phone off the hook.

The Older Man

Dating an Older Man is almost a prerequisite in the dating world. The reason for this is that when most women start to date, the guys their age are . . . well, they're total numnucks. They're immature and awkward, and their idea of sophistication is using a napkin to wipe up the milk that they made come out of their nose. And as you can imagine, a younger man's sense of humor will revolve around bodily functions. Sure, you can wait until a guy your age becomes more mature (although don't ever expect the body-humor thing to ever change), or you can save yourself years of waiting and decide to date an Older Man.

But the truth is that dating an Older Man may be riddled with more problems than pros. For example:

- An Older Man can be condescending. Because he's no doubt traveled more than you and has had more life experiences, you may feel stupid around him. He can finish the *New York Times* crossword while you struggle to complete the one in the back of *People* magazine.
- An Older Man may be going through a midlife crisis and see you more as arm candy than a real companion.
- An Older Man may have more removable body parts, like teeth and hair, than you can deal with.
- An Older Man may be overly concerned with staying regular.
- An Older Man may not be much of a partier. He has trouble staying up past midnight, and his recreational drug of choice is Viagra.

Although it isn't always the case, many women date older men because they don't have a very strong father figure. I know that's what led me to date an Older Man. My father often traveled for weeks at a time, and even when he was at home, he was never quite comfortable around kids.

Good tip

Never call an Older Man "Daddy" in the bedroom.

Because of this I fell for a man eleven years my senior, and he ended up breaking my heart. Of course, it only seems fair to blame dear old dad for my pain since I blame my mother for so many other things that have gone wrong with my life.

The Younger Man

If you're past the age of twenty-five, dating a Younger Man is seen as enticing and a little bit wicked. If you're much younger than that, the only thing it's seen as is statutory rape. The reason that younger men can be so tempting is that they're seen as more energetic than their older competitors and are more naive when it comes to love. That's because younger men don't have the same dating battle scars that years of heartache can inflict.

There's also something a bit deviant about dating a Younger Man. For some reason, society sees this type of behavior as taboo, especially if the woman is many years his senior. I'm not sure why this is the case; in fact, it goes against all logic. For one thing, a woman hits her sexual peak later in life then a man does, and for another, a woman's life expectancy is longer as well. So as it stands now, if we marry an Older Man like society wants us to, we'll be sexually frustrated and forced to spend our remaining years with only our pleasure toy to keep us company.

But even though it may go against the norm, you may decide to throw caution to the wind and find a nubile young stud to go out with. Maybe you feel like you're getting on in years and that dating a guy who has trouble growing facial hair will make you feel young again. But the truth is that it just may have the opposite effect. When a younger guy uses hip lingo like "cheddar" and "floss," you assume that he's making up his marketing list. You find yourself lecturing him about the perils of eating too much junk food and are constantly turning down his stereo. And at some point during your relationship, you should expect that someone will mistake you for his mother. If that doesn't make you feel old, nothing will.

Because of a guy's younger age, he may not be as financially stable as you would like him to be. You'll have to cough up the bucks whenever you go out simply because his paycheck from Pizza Hut doesn't cover your date. A younger guy may not dress very well and often owns only one suit that his mother bought him years ago for his cousin's bat mitzvah. And you may be reluctant to drive in his '93 Geo because the only extra feature it has is his pair of Rollerblades he keeps in the trunk.

> **Red flag**
>
> Your younger guy thinks the Surgeon General is a member of the military.

As for his apartment—well, be prepared to enter it wearing a gas mask and waders. Even though he lives in a one bedroom, he's forced to share it with half a dozen other guys in order to make the rent. There are dishes piled up in the sink, smelly clothes in every corner, and a bathroom that's like a petri dish with plumbing. And the décor . . . oh, the décor. The bookcases are stacked cinder blocks, the sofa pillows are flatter than Madonna's voice, and the only magazines there are to browse through are sold wrapped in brown paper.

And when it comes to the sex, well, it may not be all that you've imagined it to be. Sure, he has the drive and stamina of Seabiscuit, but he has other passions as well. When he asks you to play with his joystick, chances are that he's referring to the one that's attached to his Sony PlayStation. And he lacks experience because most of his knowledge of what

    " Whenever I would go to Ben's apartment, it was so disgusting that I'd spend most of my time there cleaning up. I'd buy him little knickknacks like canisters for his flour and sugar. At times, Ben seemed like less of a boyfriend and more like my son in a college dorm.**"**

                                                         —Melissa

pleases a woman comes from watching *South Park*. Sure, he's heard of a G spot before, but he thinks it's something that needs to be removed by a dermatologist.

The Noncommittal Man

The Noncommittal Man is one of the worst pariahs out there, and also one of the most difficult to recognize. He presents himself well, appears confident, and for some mysterious reason, you find that you're drawn to him right from the start. Then the mystery reveals itself as he utters the seven words that act as the strongest woman magnet in the English language: "I'm not looking for a serious relationship." WHAM! You're hooked!

    Women can be quite predictable when it comes to matters of the heart. Just as a man loves a good chase, a woman, in turn, loves a good challenge. We all have one inherent flaw that's worse than our ability to develop cellulite. It's that erroneous belief that if we meet a man who doesn't want to commit, we have the power to change his mind. We're fully convinced that the only reason that a Noncommittal Man hasn't gotten down on bended knee is that he has never met a woman who was worthy of the effort. Little do we know that the reason he hasn't bent down yet is that he suffers from emotional arthritis.

The lifespan of a relationship with a Noncommittal Man can vary. It can be as short as a few weeks or as long as a few decades. But however long it lasts, it always follows the same tumultuous path. You find your Noncommittal Man and go out a few times and get along famously. But then he doesn't pound down your door the way you had hoped, and so the dating challenge begins. You obsess about how to get him to pay more attention to you. You buy the books about "The Rules" and follow them like congress just voted them into law. You do everything they suggest, like appear disinterested when you're with him and don't return his calls right away. But instead of having him welcome you with open arms, the only thing you're greeted with when you get home is "no new messages" playing on your answering machine.

Then comes your inevitable conclusion that there must be something wrong with you and you start to give in to these feelings of unworthiness. Like the little engine that

> **"**I dated Bradley for five years hoping he'd change his mind about marriage. On Valentine's Day he told me that he had a big surprise for me. He rented a limo and took me out to an expensive romantic dinner and I was convinced that this was the night that he was finally going to propose. As it turned out, his big surprise was that he rented the limo.**"**
>
> —Jane

could, you maniacally chant "I think I can, I think I can" as you plow up the hill, determined to get him to fall in love with you. Your self-destructive wheels keep spinning, but nothing seems to work. In the end he remains noncommittal and you end up needing to be committed.

If you have enough perseverance and a strong enough pain threshold, this kind of relationship can drag on for years. It finally ends when either you're defeated enough to cut your losses or he dumps you because you've become a crazed lunatic. Either way you come out of the relationship with no ring on your

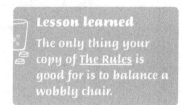

Lesson learned
The only thing your copy of _The Rules_ is good for is to balance a wobbly chair.

finger. The only good that comes from this painful ordeal is that you manage to shed a few dress sizes from wallowing in your sea of depression.

Mr. Come On Too Strong

Mr. Come On Too Strong is the kind of man that thrives on women's weakness for love, romance, and security. The pattern of a Mr. Come On Too Strong is always the same. He'll seek out a woman who interests him and has no qualms telling her that she's the one he's been looking for all of his life. He appears truthful and sincere and flatters her so much that she can't help but fall hard. By the time they have their first meal together, he's invited her to go away for a romantic weekend. And by the time that they have their first night of passion, he's told her what type of music he wants playing at their wedding and the names of all their future children.

But then somewhere between meeting his mother and deciding whether or not to take his last name, she realizes that his feelings toward her have taken a nosedive. Now, not only does he not hold her hand, he doesn't even return her phone calls. When she shows up unannounced at his door, he assures her that nothing's wrong, but deep down, she knows that there is. There's been a shift in their relationship and that shift is as big as the San Andreas Fault. Something has changed, and she stands helpless to do anything about it. Their relationship is dying and she doesn't have a clue as to why.

> **Civic duty**
>
> *Just as photos of missing children are posted on milk cartons, photos of these cruel jerks should be posted on Mallomar boxes to warn other women. Write to your senator.*

A good therapist would tell you that a Mr. Come On Too Strong has abandonment issues. He's so afraid of being left that the only thing he can do is to leave first. He loves the idea of love and security, but whenever he comes close to having it, he runs for his life and into the arms of another innocent victim. When this happens you may feel like relationship road kill, but don't ever blame yourself. The only thing that you did wrong was not to recognize the signs to begin with. But that's a mistake that you're never going to make again.

The Married Man

The reason that dating a Married Man is a bad idea is obvious: it's a lose-lose situation for all. There are only two paths that this kind of relationship can take and both of them end in disaster. One path is that he'll tell you that he loves you and plans on leaving his wife. Of course, he doesn't know exactly when this will happen because he has to wait for the timing to be just right. It's either too close to the holidays, or to his wife's birthday, or to the end of the school year, or even too close to the solar equinox.

The other path that this torrid affair can take is that he may in fact leave his wife. Or more likely, she'll leave him when she discovers that he's a two-timer. And then what do you have? You have a man who's proven himself to be a cheat. How can you ever trust such a man? And in the wake of this monstrosity are his messed up kids that are now your responsibility to raise every weekend and alternate Wednesday, and an ex-wife that's so spiteful, she makes Lorena Bobbitt look like Carol Brady.

What to do when you finally wise up
Wait until he falls asleep and write "He's all yours!" on his ass in permanent marker.

If you think about it, why should a Married Man who's having an affair ever leave his wife at all when he has the best of both worlds? He has a woman at home who cooks for him, cares for his children, and washes the skid marks out of his boxers. And then he has you on the side to wear all the trashy lingerie that his wife refuses to wear. So you'll hang on year after year, waking up alone every morning and praying that he can slip away every night to give you the fix that you so desperately need. And in the end you'll realize that you've wasted the best and most wrinkle-free years of your life on a man who has strung you along like a pull toy.

The Divorced Man with Kids

It's bound to happen at one time or another. Because of the high rate of divorce, your chances of falling for a man who has kids is about the same as getting your period on the day you wear your white linen skirt. Sure, you may be reluctant at first to get involved with such a man. Dating him may feel like you're buying a used car. It may look okay on the outside, but you don't know what problems await you under the hood. But at least this guy has one thing going for him that most every guy that you've fallen for doesn't. He's proven himself to be able to commit. A guy who's been married understands the joys of having someone there when he gets home. He appreciates having a wife listen to him talk about his problems at work. And the fact that he has regular sex and a drawer full of clean socks doesn't hurt either.

The big problem that you're going to face with such a man is the kids. Because of the strong guilt he feels for ending the marriage and traumatizing his offspring, he indulges their every whim. No matter how many times you play with his kids, you can never get in their good graces. And even though their dad sees you as a caring woman with a nice ass, the kids see you as a threat to getting their parents back together and the reason that they get less attention from their father.

Whenever the kids are around, their needs will always come first. Although you understand why this is so, it still doesn't bother you any less. Sure kids can be precious sweet angels, but they can also be destructive, manipulative brats who know how to play their daddy like their overabundance of Fisher-Price toys they've been given to stop their tantrums. They know how to get anything they want, and the cold hard truth is that they don't want you.

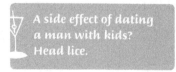

A side effect of dating a man with kids? Head lice.

But if your idea of a romantic dinner is a slice at Chuck E. Cheese's, and you don't mind cleaning up projectile vomit and sticky floors covered with grape jelly, then go right ahead and date Divorced Man with Kids. Who knows, maybe you can learn how to bribe these rugrats into liking you with M&Ms and Beanie Babies. But chances are in time, the only thing that you'll learn from dating Divorced Man with Kids is that you've bitten off more Tater Tots than you can chew.

The Player

The term "Player" says it all, for when it comes to matters of love and romance, a Player sees it all as just one big game. This kind of man has only one goal in mind: He wants to come out of the game a winner no matter who gets hurt. And how does a Player win? By scoring, of course . . . with as many women as possible.

The Player is an exciting and attractive breed, as well as a very skilled opponent. After years of sitting on the side-lines studying his worthy opponents, the Player has learned enough about the game to make it in the big leagues. He wears the right clothes, has the right job, and drives the right car. He's funny and charismatic and knows how to lure a woman into the game by simply raising a seductive eye-brow. Once he finds a qualified opponent (which is basically anyone with 2 X chromosomes), he hears the starting bell and the clock starts to tick.

Since a true Player knows that there's no "I" in TEAM, he surrounds himself with other professionals. No matter how crowded the bar is, he knows the bartender, so he'll be assured of getting you a drink. No matter how overbooked the restaurant, he knows the maitre d', so he'll be able to impress you by getting a good table. Because of his circle of loyal team members, a Player can get into the hippest clubs and backstage to the hottest concerts wearing only his brilliant, whitened smile.

A Player makes you feel like you're special, but what you don't know is that you're not the only woman that he's playing with. Players have learned how to adeptly juggle several opponents at one time. If you notice, a Player tends to cancel on you at the last minute. He'll tell you that he's working late or that he's not feeling well, but what's really happened is that he met a new opponent with longer legs and wanted to upgrade.

Sweet revenge

Place a personal ad on behalf of the Player with his name and address, stating that he longs to meet a woman who's averse to personal hygiene.

Once you feel a Player start to distance himself from you, you do what any other red-blooded American girl who is trying to keep a man would do: sleep with him. The difference is that while you see fireworks, he only hears the final buzzer. The game is over and he came out the winner. And now that he's won the game, he moves on to his next game of the series in his perpetual quest to play in the Super Bowl of love.

Mr. God's Gift to Women

One day it's bound to happen. A man will approach you wearing an air of confidence and far too much cologne. His shirt is unbuttoned to his navel, he's dripping in gaudy jewelry, and he uses so many hair products that it's stiff enough to slice deli meat. He uses a full line of male facial products and, if you look closely, you may notice his eyebrows have even been waxed. This, my friend, is Mr. God's Gift to Women, and you've just met the ultimate narcissist.

Mr. God's Gift to Women will give you the impression that you're being blessed by his divine presence as if he were the pope and you were some ailing devout Catholic wanting to be saved. He'll try to get you to go out with him by using his powers of persuasion. Unfortunately his powers are like that of a diesel Volvo chugging to climb up a steep mountain.

As easily as Mr. God's Gift to Women can be recognized by his physical characteristics, he can also be recognized by his personality traits. Seeing him in action will remind you of Steve Martin in those old "Two Wild and Crazy Guys" sketches on *Saturday Night Live.* Within minutes of meeting you, he'll try to

Red flag
He carries pictures of himself in his wallet.

impress you with his new BlackBerry and his feng shui condominium. After that, he'll fill you in on all aspects of his most favorite topic: himself. Oh what fun!

A Mr. God's Gift to Women isn't just born, he's made. He's no doubt a product of being an only child raised by a mother who smothered him with too much love. This behavior led him to think that he was actually more special than he truly was. As a result, he now thinks he's the greatest thing to happen to women since stretch jeans. Because of his misled ego, he won't go out with any woman who thinks otherwise. And you can forget about making a good impression on his mother. As you can guess, no one will ever be good enough for her precious son, and chances are that he'll remain a BFL (bachelor for life).

Mr. Great Guy with No Sex Appeal

At least once in your dating life you meet a guy who has
many of the qualities that you've been looking for in a man.
He's funny, he's bright, and most of all, he absolutely adores
you. He loves your quirky earrings that no one else seems to
appreciate. He laughs at your sarcastic wit that most people
find offensive. And he's the only person that you've ever met
who shares your passion for *My So-Called Life* reruns. You
want more than anything to fall for this guy, but there's one
thing that stands in your way: You feel absolutely no attraction toward him whatsoever.

I've been there once myself and I know how frustrating
this situation can be. I met a Mr. Great Guy with No Sex
Appeal once who seemed perfect for me. He was creative
and intelligent, and wanted nothing more than to please me.
He wrote me beautiful love letters, brought me my favorite
flowers, and took me to wonderful places. Not only did I
enjoy his company, but also you could tell that he adored me
because he glowed like a Halloween pumpkin whenever he
was in my presence.

But the fact that I wasn't attracted to this man was caus-
ing a problem. After dating for a while, I sensed that he
wanted to sleep together. I sensed this because he told me
that at least a zillion times. But no matter how much I tried,
I just couldn't force myself to do it. I used every excuse in
the book for postponing the inevitable, and then made up
a few of my own. Once I told him that I couldn't possibly
have sex with him because it was so hot outside. So when
he came over the next day with a carful of fans, I knew
that I couldn't hold him off any longer. I did what any girl
would do: get drunk. I had more margaritas than a Spanish

phonebook. I was like a Boy Scout with wet sticks desperately trying to ignite even the smallest of flames, but it was futile. Had it not been for the margaritas I would have ended it right then and there. But good old Maggie gave me the incentive I needed to keep on keeping on.

When it was over I decided that it was the worst sex that I've ever had. I felt absolutely nothing at all. No closeness. No connection. Nothing. I remember thinking that if I ever were to get married and my husband told me he had an affair but that it didn't mean anything, I'd know exactly what he meant.

After that experience I realized that our relationship couldn't go anywhere. I told him that I couldn't see him anymore. I used the excuse that I wasn't over my last boyfriend. After all, he was a nice guy and he did buy me all those fans.

For me, this kind of relationship with a wonderful, yet spark-free kind of man, can be the most infuriating of them all. You're like the ugly stepsister desperate to get that itty-bitty glass slipper to fit over your large foot. You're so close to getting the man of your dreams that you keep struggling to make things work, but in the end all you get is a foot full of bunions.

Friendly advice
As much as a man like this is a great boost to your ego, don't keep him around as a friend. It's just plain mean.

Through this experience I learned that there has to be at least some attraction in order to have a physical relationship with a man. I know that I said women have evolved past a man's looks and now search for more substantial things, but there has to be at least a little bit of chemistry. I'm not saying that you need as much as in a meth lab, just as much as in those kiddie sets that let you build your own volcano.

Mr. Manly Man

If you feel an odd attraction to the Brawny Man, this type of guy may be just what you're looking for. He's rugged and handsome and looks great in a tool belt. He loves to do macho things like fly-fish, play poker with the boys, and build things around the house, maybe even the house itself. He decorates with trophies and stuffed critters that he snared during his many hunting expeditions.

If you date Mr. Manly Man, you'll find that everyone you know will accept him. Your gal pals will adore him in that primeval caveman/cavewoman kind of way. Your guy friends will admire him because of his ability to grow a thick beard overnight. Even your gay friends will be drawn to him since he looks like a man that's been redone by the team from *Queer Eye for the Straight Guy*.

Hold off on dumping him . . .

Until he's installed dimmers for all your light switches and built you a nice set of shelves.

The problem is, what Mr. Manly Man has in brute force he lacks in brain matter. I don't mean to say that he's dumb. In fact, he has a lot of knowledge stored in that oversized head of his, but it may not be the kind of knowledge that you find interesting. He can't name all fifty states, but he can recite the official colors of every team in the NFL.

A problem you may face with a Manly Man is that he doesn't believe that the sexes are equal. After you hook up, he won't want you to pursue your career. Rather, he'd prefer that you stay barefoot and pregnant with your main chore being that you keep the refrigerator stocked with brewskies.

The Bad Boy

This breed of man is the most dangerous and notorious of them all. But, admittedly, he is also the most fun. When you think of a Bad Boy you conjure up visions of a man climbing onto a Harley Davidson with a cigarette dangling from his lips. He has multiple tattoos and so many piercings that you can use his body to drain spaghetti. But the truth is that any guy without a pocket protector and flood pants could be a Bad Boy candidate. He doesn't have to own a leather jacket or refuse to have a steady job. He could walk among us and blend quite well into any crowd. The main requirement for him to qualify as a Bad Boy is that you're painfully attracted to him and that he treats you like crap.

The reason the Bad Boy is such a powerful force to be reckoned with is that he's actually two kinds of men put together. He's a unique combination of the Noncommittal Man and the Player, and this is a more enticing combination than peanut butter and chocolate. But unlike the Noncommittal Man and the Player, the Bad Boy has an edge to him. He takes risks and is not afraid of being caught. Being with him fills your body with the same kind of adrenaline that you had as a kid when you stole a Snickers bar from a drugstore. But instead of staying up all night waiting for the police to come, you're up for a different reason: because *you* will. Yes, sex with a Bad Boy will no doubt be the best sex of your life. It's hot and wild and extremely passionate. But although a Bad Boy is good in your bed, he's also bad in your life, and you'll almost always wind up getting hurt.

As much as it pains you, a Bad Boy makes no claims of wanting to get married and have kids. He doesn't dream of having a white picket fence or even of being in a serious relationship. What he does want is to keep you dangling from a thread and available whenever the mood suits him. You're forever struggling to tame him into something that he will never be. He gives you the least amount of attention and you feed off of it for weeks. But you can't have more until he says so and you're left feeling helpless and obsessed.

Dating a Bad Boy is a necessity if you're ever truly going to fall in love, because he acts as your barometer for all future men. Although getting over him can be tough, you can be assured that you'll learn a lot from the experience. For one thing, you can see how bad it feels to be with a man who doesn't give you what you need, so you will appreciate it when you get a man who does. For another thing, you'll learn how low your self-esteem has to plummet before you put an end to your emotional abuse. For some women, this lesson can take years to learn and even when they've finally managed to break free, they find another Bad Boy to take the last one's place.

How to get over him

Watch Rebel Without a Cause until you want to vomit. It's the method Schick Centers used to help smokers quit and it fared pretty well for them.

Mr. Passive Man

My friend Allison's biggest complaint about dating is that all the men she meets are too passive. They can never take a stand on an issue or make up their minds about a situation no matter how trivial it is. She says they're the kind of men that would make horrible boyfriends, although she admits they'd make a fantastic jury if she were ever to be accused of a crime.

Maybe you know what Allison is going through. Maybe you, too, are tired of dating men who have a backbone as strong as Play-Doh. They have absolutely no desire to be the instigator of the relationship and instead choose to be submissive. You can disagree with me if you want and send me nasty letters, but I believe that most women don't want a guy that's wishy-washy. There's a feeling of safety you get when you're with a strong, confident man who doesn't keel over with indecisiveness whenever he looks at a wine list.

> **Red flags**
> He'll take an eternity to decide which of the thirty-one flavors to order at Baskin-Robbins.

A typical date with a Passive Man will go something like this: He'll ask you out to dinner but wants you to choose the restaurant because he can't handle the pressure. He'll pick you up but will refuse to decide what music to listen to on the way there. You'll ask him if he wants to split a desert and he'll say, "Sure, whatever you want to order is fine with me." You're making so many decisions that by the end of the evening you're not only growing impatient, you're also growing balls.

Even though passive men are mushy, there are some benefits to being with them. You get to see all the chick flicks you want. If you ever move in together you can decorate the whole place in pink floral prints. And you get to control the remote so you can watch all the girly shows that you would be far too embarrassed to watch with your past boyfriends. As for Allison, she'll pass on those benefits no matter how fond she is of pink floral, and she'll continue her search for a man that she can't dominate. I wish her luck, because considering that she's over six feet tall, she's going to dominate the majority of them.

Reasons Why Having a Dog Can Be
So Much Better Than Having a Boyfriend

1. He's always excited to see you when you get home from work.
2. He willingly cuddles with you in bed.
3. When you're with him, you don't have to suck in your stomach because you're bloated.
4. He encourages you to get out of the house and take a walk.
5. He doesn't cheat.
6. He eats anything you make for him.
7. He doesn't pressure you to have sex . . . unless you count the occasional leg humping.
8. He doesn't care if you forget to put on your deodorant. In fact, he'd prefer it.
9. He doesn't hate your mother.
10. He'll want to be with you until the day he dies . . . unless, of course, he sees a squirrel; then he'll want to bolt.

chapter three

where to dive into the dating pool so you won't break your neck

I've heard many different theories about how to find love.
One is that you can expect to find it when you least expect it.
Another is that you can find love in the most unusual places.
I'm sure that all these theories have merit except for the one
I heard about how you'll find love as soon as you stop looking. This theory never made sense to me because I'm a firm
believer in going out and getting what you want. I for one
have never found my lost car keys just by sitting on my ass
and I certainly never found a boyfriend by doing so. Therefore, as much as dating sucks, sometimes a girl's just gotta
get off her bootie to find a boyfriend.

I know the thought of putting yourself out there does
more harm to your stomach than Splenda, but you really
have no other choice if you want to improve your chances of
finding love. I remember years ago I got a speeding ticket
and had to go to traffic school to have it erased from my
record. So I went down the list of classes I could take, and

even though every part of me wanted to sign up for "Lettuce Amuse You Traffic School," I forced myself to sign up for the one that was designed for singles. I wish that I could tell you that I met the man of my dreams at that class, but the only thing I got out of it was the erased ticket; well, actually, I also learned the two things that you can throw out of a car that are not considered littering.

So if you want to find love, where should you look? The truth is that there are several places to choose from. To make it even easier, I've compiled a list of the most current and successful methods that you can use to try to meet your one true love. All of these methods vary. Some of them cost thousands of dollars, while others are free. Some have been around hundreds of years, while others gained popularity along with Uggs. Oh, in case you're curious, the two things that you can throw out your window that are not considered littering are water and the feathers off a live chicken. See, now aren't these precious pieces of trivia worth getting your lazy ass out of your La-Z-Boy?

Where Everybody Knows Your Name

Let's face it. Alcohol is to dating what a spoonful of sugar is to medicine. And despite the hangovers, foggy memories, and other messy ailments, millions upon millions of young single Americans head to their favorite bars every weekend to let off some steam, have a few cocktails, and flirt like crazy.

As you make your way through the bar's nicotine fog, you can feel the guys giving you the once-over. You are but a walking piece of meat and these butchers are deciding whether you're prime cut or ground round. Treat the walk from the door to the bar as your own red carpet moment. All eyes will be on you, and it is your time to shine. So use it wisely. Walk tall, stand proud, and scope the crowd to see if there's anyone who catches your eye.

When frequenting a bar, keep in mind that men flock to them because they're a place where boys can be boys. They can bond over a close game, play a few rounds of pool, and, of course, get mind-numbingly drunk. So beware. Although bars can be an easy place to meet a man, you have to be very cautious of the kind of man that you can meet. It's important to remember that men don't go to bars to meet a wife. Any man you meet there is thinking in terms of a short-term relationship. Very short term. Their most optimistic hope for the evening is not to say, "Will you do me the honor of being my wife?" but to slur the words "Will you do me?"

While some lucky few do manage to meet in bars and live happily ever after, don't get your hopes up. The most that you should expect in your evening is to meet an ogre or two with beer breath and wandering hands. There are a couple of things, however, that you can do to improve your odds of meeting a prince rather than an ogre.

1. You've heard the expression that timing is everything, and this is certainly true for a girl's night out. The best time to get to a bar is when it is moderately crowded, usually around 6:00 for a happy hour or 10:00 for a Saturday night. If you get there too early, people who walk in see you but don't have enough liquid courage to say hello. Once they've been there for a while and have loosened up a bit, you're already old news and they're focused on the next hot thing coming in the door. Remember, they don't call it a meat market for nothing, and everyone

wants the freshest cut. But if you get there too late, all of the barstools and tables will be taken, and the men will probably have had too much to drink to have a legitimate conversation.

2. Keep in mind that no matter how great the guy seems, he is still a stranger. Unlike a setup by friends, guys you meet in bars have no pedigree. You can't call anyone you know to check his history or personality. It is the ultimate crapshoot, which is why it often has a crappy ending.

No Pain, No Gain

Gyms have always been a place to build up your social life as well as your abs. And now that the obesity rate is at an all-time high, so is the amount of guys with gym memberships. Besides just being a serious place to work on your flab, gyms may also be a great place to meet someone fabulous.

One of the best parts about scoping out men at the gym is that you don't have that feeling of desperation that you have at a bar or party when you have to act fast for fear of never seeing a certain guy again. If you're a member of a gym, you usually work out at a regular schedule and tend to see a lot of the same faces (and abs and butts) when you go. Because of this, if you didn't have an instant love connection with the cute guy on the Gravitron, you can always try again when he's doing the downward dog next to you in Thursday's yoga class.

Because of the nature of the gym, there are plenty of things to talk about besides your astrological sign. There is always some new piece of equipment or new exercise class to critique. Or you can talk about the latest diet or health craze or why wheat grass tastes like feet. This way if someone wants to meet you, there are ample conversation starters.

Still better is that if a guy asks you out at the gym, you don't have to feel insecure about your looks when he comes to pick you up. He's already seen you at your very worst with stringy hair and no makeup. You should feel confident that you can only go up on the looks scale from here. Also, you can check him out more thoroughly than you could if you were to meet him elsewhere. You can see if he has six-pack abs or a soft belly caused by drinking too many six packs. You can check out his back for hair, and if he wears those tight biker shorts, you can even see if he's circumcised.

Even though there are some advantages to dating someone you meet at the gym, there is one major drawback: If you go out with a fellow gym member and he turns out to be a loser, you still have to see him when you work out. This can turn your once-sacred oasis into a place where the most exercise you get is toning your thighs from ducking for cover. And even though you may find a guy or two that you're interested in at your gym, by far the vast majority of them will be your usual dimwits who join a gym solely to watch women work out on the inner-thigh machine.

Where to Find a Man with a Good Hard Drive

In the past decade there has been an explosion in the amount of online dating sites that are available on the Internet. Although there are the standard sites like Match.com and eHarmony.com that appeal to your average middle-class young professional, there are a host of other sites that are guaranteed to fit your every need. There are religious dating sites, ethnic dating sites, interracial dating sites, triple X adult dating sites, and S&M dating sites. It doesn't matter if you're a swinging single or a married swinger, there's a site to suit your needs.

Although there are variations among the different dating Web sites, the basic principles remain the same. As a member you pay a nominal fee, pick a screen name to protect your anonymity, write a profile about yourself stating your basic personality traits and interests, and select characteristics that you want in a mate. You then post a photo of yourself and pray to God that no one you know will recognize you. Some people find that setting up a profile can be a degrading ordeal, sort of like posting yourself on some sort of list. But instead of a "Most Wanted" list it's more like a "Most Pathetic" list.

After the setup is complete, the virtual dating begins. You scroll down the list of available men and pick and choose the ones you like as if you were selecting items from a dim sum menu. After you check off the ones you want, you wait to see if they find you appetizing as well. You resist the temptation to go online during every commercial break to check your in-box. Finally, when you can take it no more, you log on to see who has responded to your request. You hold your breath knowing full well that your mood will change one way or the other in the next millisecond. For your in-box is as powerful a tool as your bathroom scale in determining whether your ego will soar out of the stratosphere or plummet into that dark place reserved for Phish Food ice cream.

As with most things in life, there is the good side as well as a bad side. One good thing about cyberdating is that it's a great way to meet someone that involves a minimum amount of effort. How else can you find the man of your dreams in the comfort of your home unless, of course, you live at Melrose Place. Another plus is the way that the system is set up. All you need to do is scroll down the list of available profiles and point and click your way to romance. In fact, it's just like any other online shopping site like J. Crew or The Gap, but instead of getting a dream outfit, you're getting a dreamboat.

On the flip side, there are some negative aspects to dating online. The most common one is the rejection factor. Even though you never met your cyberstud face to face, it still hurts when you get his message that he's not interested in going out with you. It hurts even more when he doesn't even give you the courtesy of responding to your message at all. You sit and wait and tell yourself that he just hasn't read the message yet, when you know full well that he's logged on seven times since you sent it. This, my friend, is the Internet version of being stood up. Because there are so many online bachelors, there are plenty of opportunities for this kind of rejection. It seems that you have to develop a thick skin when you date online, and that skin needs to be as thick as Donatella Versace.

But the biggest negative aspect of cyberdating is the false sense of closeness that develops after you've hooked up with someone online and instant-messaged them for hours. Because of the anonymity factor, you're more likely to share intimate details with this stranger than you would if you had just met for drinks. This false sense of closeness makes you fall deeper and faster for a guy that you hardly know, and you develop unrealistic, high expectations like "this could be it!" Then when you finally do meet your cybersweetie, your chances of getting hurt are much greater. And for that matter, so are your chances of sleeping with him. Therefore, when you finally do meet in person, *don't* wear your heart on your sleeve, but *do* wear an embarrassing pair of granny underpants.

Although most cyberdating Web sites are pretty straight-forward, there are some basic things that you'll want to know before you let your fingers do the stalking:

- If you're going to post a photograph of yourself, you should use one that's realistic. Sure you may be tempted to hire a professional to give you that wind-blown, airbrushed effect, but this can only lead to rejection down the road.
- On this same note, you should know that men can fake it too when it comes to creating their personal profile. For instance, you should automatically sub-tract two inches from their posted height and 30 per-cent from their annual income.
- You should always check out the new listings first when you go online. These guys get snatched off the shelf faster than the latest new listing at the video store.

After all is said and done, cyberdating can be a decent way to meet that special someone, as long as you don't take it all so seriously. You'd be a fool not to take advantage of living in an age when you can get anything you want online from a spatula to a spouse. And if you don't end up living happily ever after, you can also use the Internet to get a quickie cyberdivorce.

Find Me a Find, Catch Me a Catch

Although matchmakers have been "finding a find and catch-ing a catch" for hundreds of years, they've been getting even more recognition over the past few decades. The Internet has hundreds of matchmaker Web sites. There are television shows like Miss Matched that parody the life of one of the most famous matchmakers, Samantha Daniels. And, of course, there are movies made about them like my all-time favorite *Crossing Delancey*. If you haven't seen this 1988 film, it's definitely worth renting. In the movie, a Jewish matchmaker sets up Isabelle (Amy Irving) with a pickle maker named Sam (Peter Riegert). At first she rejects this funny little gherkin, but in the end she realizes that there's more to him than she thought, and she ends up relishing him.

I know a thing or two about matchmakers myself. I used one years ago when my Aunt Rhoda passed away. My Aunt Rhoda was the character in the family. She was loud and obnoxious and everyone adored her. When I was little, she would always have a cigarette in one hand and my ass in the other, which she would constantly squeeze.

Anyway, Aunt Rhoda left me some money and I thought the best way to honor her was to use it to hire a matchmaker since she would always tell me that she couldn't wait until I found a good man and settled down. I should have just used the money as toilet paper since it ended up going down the drain anyway. Since I didn't know the first thing about matchmakers, I chose one who called herself "The Beverly Hills Matchmaker." I should have gotten my first clue that she was a rip-off artist when her office was located in Culver City. I filled out a questionnaire, had a photo taken, and went home to wait for the phone to ring. Oh, it rang all right. I felt like a couple of Lakers playoff seats, because there were men after me right and left. Although I felt flattered at first, once I went out with these guys I realized why they were so desperate. They were the biggest group of losers since the Cubs.

Not all matchmakers use the same strategies when it comes to making matches. Some of them are actually more like a personal shopper. You tell them exactly what kind of man you're looking for and they'll scour the city to find an exact fit. But instead of winding up with a black cocktail dress that's drop-dead gorgeous, you hope to end up with a man that is. As you can see, a matchmaker of this type can be the perfect solution for busy people who don't have much free time to shop for themselves, whether it be for suits or for suitors.

When it comes to selecting a matchmaker, it's vital that you do your homework first. You need to find out how a matchmaker operates, what you can expect to get for your money, and a list of qualified references. When it comes to matchmakers, not all are created equal. Some have been around for years and have wonderful reputations, while others see matchmaking as a quick way to make a fast buck. Some charge hefty fees for their services while others only charge fees to the men. And, like most everything else in life, you really do get what you pay for. Sure, you can buy cheap when it comes to a package of cotton balls, but when it comes to finding a life partner, you really shouldn't scrimp.

In God We Trust

Belonging to a church or a temple gives you more than a place to worship God. It also gives you a place to meet Mr. Right. Or Mr. Right-binowitz. Or Mr. Right-McGinty. That's because if a guy is a member of a religious sect, chances are that he has a better sense of values and morals than a

Mr. Right Off the Street. It seems that being a good person is sort of a prerequisite to having God in your life.

Most religious congregations encourage their members to date—assuming, of course, that they're not married. They know that becoming husband and wife and going forth and multiplying are what God intended for us to do. They also know that being married increases one's net worth and therefore they're able to have more coins tossed into their collection plate. Communion wafers don't grow on trees you know.

Because of their interest in pairing you off like the animals on Noah's Ark, these houses of worship offer singles events to help encourage the process. These mixers are intended to provide a relaxing environment for singles to meet one another. They take place at the house of worship so that the atmosphere is friendly and the pressure is minimal—and, if you do anything immoral or unethical, there is a confessional conveniently located.

Unfortunately, many people who attend these mixers find them to be a huge waste of time. One of the inherent problems is that most of the guys that go to these functions are the same one's that you'd see every Sunday. If there are no sparks after being preached to that the world is coming to an end, the chances of igniting passion over a platter of cocktail franks is pretty much nil.

The main advantage of being with someone who shares the same religious beliefs that you do is that they better understand some of the unusual behaviors that you may demonstrate. For instance, if your religion prohibits you from eating certain foods, using certain prophylactics, or even operating heavy machinery on certain days, other guys may think you're a freak. But ones who are members of your same religion will be abstaining from shellfish, condoms, or forklifts right along with you.

The truth is that most congregational events for singles have gotten a bad reputation. They're thought of as being depressing and dull. The atmosphere tends to be solemn, the food tends to be bland, the alcohol tends to be absent, and the music tends to be so dull that you wish they'd play Yanni just to liven things up. But even with all that, if you're a nice religious girl looking for a nice religious boy, you might as well give it a try. Who knows, maybe by some miracle you'll meet the man of your dreams. And if you think about it, being in a house of worship is the best place for miracles to occur!

Working It!

Although there are some pitfalls when it comes to dating someone at the workplace, it's a method that's worked well for me in the past. Because work isn't thought of as a dating environment, my coworkers and I didn't flirt, didn't worry about what was in our teeth, and didn't stammer to make awkward conversation—except, of course, when we were asking the boss for a raise. Instead, we got to know each other as we really were, without playing games or following "rules." And, because our job was so intense, with long hours, incredible stress, and lots of abuse from our hostile boss, we bonded with the intensity of Grandma's denture adhesive. We became quick friends and sometimes even quicker lovers simply because we worked, ate, and struggled together side by side.

If you're ever involved in a relationship at work, you'll find that office romances progress faster than the nonoffice kind. You aren't waiting by the phone for them to call or seeing them only on the weekend. You're with them Monday thru Friday, from morning till night. You take coffee breaks together, share lunch hours, and even send each other dirty little e-mails. As it turns out, seeing someone at work is like concentrated dating.

Because of this, you develop a strong friendship with your office romances. They put their arms around you whenever you're up against a tight deadline. They make you laugh by giving you a Xerox of some embarrassing body part. And they make you cute gifts like paperclip necklaces, rubber band balls, and other trinkets made out of office supplies.

But even though your office can be a great way to get a passion as well as a pension, there are specific guidelines to follow:

- If you're going to date a coworker, date one that's on the same rung on the corporate ladder as you are. For instance, do not date your boss! Doing so appears like you have an ulterior motive, like getting a corner office as well as a boyfriend.

- Just as important, avoid dating an underling. It can be tricky to get a relationship off the ground when you have more power and pay than he does. Plus, it won't do your relationship any good if you ever have to fire the guy.

- If you start dating someone at work, keep it to yourself for as long as possible. Not only does this dissuade office gossip until the relationship is better established, it also adds to the fun!

- Be careful of sexual harassment. Office flirtations could lead to other things besides romance. They could lead to lawsuits.

Even though dating someone that you work with can be a wonderful way to find romance, it can be devastating if the relationship ends badly. If you end up getting your heart broken, be prepared for it to hemorrhage every day as you watch your ex-lover flirt with a new staff member with a better and younger resume. Not only is this bad for your mental health, but it may be bad for your career as well, since you may be so distraught that you have to look for a job elsewhere.

Blind Dating

We've all shared the experience of walking into a crowded bar, looking anxiously for the son of our mother's best friend's personal trainer's hairdresser. And once you find him, you realize that, despite the sign out front, it will definitely not be a "happy hour." Blind dating is, after all, one big crap-shoot.

Even though their chances of success are very slim, I always believed in blind dates myself and felt that they were well worth the effort. My parents met on a blind date fifty years ago, so I always remained optimistic. I kept my fingers crossed that I had inherited this luck to make up for my bulbous nose and ability to burn without ever tanning. Unfortunately, luck must skip a generation, because the only thing that I ever got out of my blind dates was the enormous desire to actually be blind so I didn't have to see the losers I was set up with.

By far the worst part about a blind date is that it reeks with awkwardness, and this awkwardness begins from your very first conversation. He'll call and you'll struggle to make witty conversation with this complete stranger. This goes on for a short period of time until he sees an opportunity to ask you out. You gotta admit this is a cake walk for the guy since he already knows he's been preapproved. For men, blind dates are basically a rejection-free Get Out of Jail card.

The next awkward moment takes place when you arrive at the location of the date and you try to recognize some guy that you've never seen before. As you walk toward the bar, you look at the various single men, hoping that someone will claim you like a lost puppy at the pound. Once at the bar, you can relax, order a stiff drink, and watch the front door for men to arrive. As they do, you converse with the Big Man upstairs, pleading, "Please God, don't let that be him" or "I beg of you! Not that guy with the mullet cut!" Occasionally, a hottie will enter and you promise God that if he's your date, your next car will be a hybrid!

And then it happens. A guy enters who looks like a lost puppy himself. You don't think that could possibly be your date because he told you that he looks like Tom Cruise and this guy looks more like Tom Arnold. As he makes his way to the bar you pretend to be engrossed in a nearby cocktail napkin. Unfortunately he sees past the façade, introduces himself as your date for the evening, and the date begins.

It doesn't take but a moment for you to talk about the one thing that you both have in common: the person who set you up. But soon the conversation runs dry and you've reached the next awkward point of the evening: the pause in the conversation. To tell you the truth, it's a pause about the size of the Grand Canyon and just as impossible to cross. You sit there, suspended in time, desperate for one of you to say even the most trivial of words to unlock you from this prison. Fortunately the hostess arrives and takes you to your table.

After a little more time in hell, the waiter comes by to take your order. It's then that you make your next plea to God and beg him that your date doesn't ask for more time or order an appetizer. God grants you this one and when the food finally arrives, you scarf it down as quickly as possible, risking asphyxiation with every bite just to end the date as quickly as possible. He on the other hand, chews his food with the speed of a DMV line.

If you partake in blind dates, but want to take out as much suffering as possible, I advise you to do the following:

- Try to make the date as short as possible. Maybe meet for a drink or coffee or better yet, arrange to drive through an intersection at the same time and wave hello. Or you could combine your date with a weekend errand like hooking up at the ATM to deposit your paycheck or meeting at Bed Bath & Beyond to get that terry cloth bath pillow that you've been putting off buying. At least if the date doesn't work out, you're able to check a few things off your to-do list.

66 I went on a blind date last month with this guy that does the voices for cartoons. The lowest point of the evening was when the cute waiter came by to take our order and my date ordered his whole meal sounding like Donald Duck. 99

—Cindi

- If possible, take along the friend who set you up. This makes for less awkward conversation, and if you have a horrible time, you take your friend down right along with you.
- Decide in advance if you want to be the first one to arrive at the location or the last. I prefer to arrive last so I don't have to sit there looking like an idiot, but others disagree. They like to get to the location early so they have time to get boozed up.

Nuptial Nookie

It's happened to us all. We get our mail and notice that over-sized envelope with our name inscribed in calligraphy. We figure that we've either been invited to yet another wedding or that we just received a letter from Mozart. Panic sets in as we discover that another precious single friend is abandoning us. From now on our conversations with her will consist of toaster ovens and inlay tile and phrases like "my husband prefers me in blue." And just when we thought we couldn't get any more depressed, we notice that there is no "plus one" next to our name. We will therefore be forced to sit at the table of misfits with all the other losers of love who are at the bottom of the romantic food chain.

Once you get over the shock, you need to look at this situation from a brand-new perspective. You need to see this as an opportunity to spend time with your oldest and dearest friends, and to witness this loving couple recite their vows to God. And you need to see it as a chance to get laid. For the fact is that many singles go to weddings and find more than just candy-coated almonds. They also find true love. If you don't believe me, just ask Monica and Chandler.

There are various reasons why this phenomenon occurs. For one, weddings take place at gloriously romantic settings. There are string quartets that play Chopin in D minor. English roses abound, scenting the air with their magnificent aroma. And bubbly champagne is served on silver trays by strapping men in sexy tuxedos. It's as if you've become a character in a Merchant-Ivory film.

Another reason for all that nuptial nookie is that weddings put you in the mood for love. You've showered and powdered and perfumed your body and squeezed it into a pastel chiffon number that accentuates all of your positives. That is, of course, unless you're one of the bridesmaids, in which case you're wearing something that makes you look like someone who has lost her sheep.

Another reason that Cupid is working overtime is that you may have just traveled a long distance to attend the wedding. This provides you an adventurous traveler's mentality that you don't get by just taking a freeway off-ramp. You figure since you've spent a few hundred bucks on a plane ticket, you're going to get something more that just some salted peanuts. And even if you didn't travel a far distance, chances are plenty of eligible bachelors have and are more than happy to give you permission to board their aircraft.

When you take all of these reasons into account, you're a girl on a mission who longs to be in the missionary position. And since the happy couple has invited plenty of single family members and friends, a lucky participant isn't far away. Best of all, unlike the men that you meet elsewhere, you can easily check out the background of these guys. Chances are he'll be given high praise since people are always anxious to pair off couples at a wedding so that they can attend yet another function with an open bar.

If you do meet someone that you're interested in going out with, do yourself a favor and steer clear of catching the bridal bouquet. If your fella catches even one glimpse of you holding onto it, he'll freak out and run far, far away. Bubbly champagne can only do so much to relax a person.

Speed Dating: Dating at the Speed of Fright

Anyone who's old enough to remember playing with Clackers may also remember the classic Neil Simon film Chapter Two. In it there's a scene where James Caan calls a woman and asks her out on a five-minute date. Most people in the theater thought this idea was rather comical, but I wasn't laughing. Instead, I was inspired by the genius of it all. I guess I was a visionary, because what was once seen as comical is now seen as commonplace due to the relatively new practice of speed dating.

The brilliance behind speed dating is that you have an opportunity to meet dozens of professional, attractive, and interesting men in just an hour or two. This speed-dating event usually takes place at a large bar or a restaurant, which is good because liquid relaxation is readily available. Other speed-dating events may take place in churches or community centers, but the mood there is much more somber and sober, because after all, God is watching.

In theory, speed dating sounds like a walk in the park, but I found it to be more like a fast sprint on sand. Many of these events are not well organized so it can take over an hour for people to check in and for the program to begin.

When the event finally does start, it's very much like a cattle call. Everyone is assigned a number, and the dating director organizes the event so that you move from table to table, man to man, learning everything that you can about a complete stranger in just a few minutes.

One of the worst things about the evening is that you're forced to tell the same story about yourself over and over and over again. And even worse, you're forced to listen to one boring background story after another. If you were just hanging out in a bar, you could politely walk away. But here you're forced to sit and listen to the mind-numbing details of what college some guy went to and feign interest. You pass the time counting the emergency exits while maintaining a frozen Miss America smile. Then, like a boxer in a ring, you're saved when the bell rings and you have but a moment to rest before starting another gruesome round.

When this bell rings, either the men stay in the same seat and the women rotate or vice versa. As the night progresses, you keep tally of the men that you'd like to see again on your scorecard and hand it in at the end. Considering the dozens of available men in the room, your list is shockingly small. Let's face it, that can't come as much of a surprise when you're in a roomful of men whose idea of dressing to impress is showing up in their best Jeff Gordon tank top.

Despite the drawbacks that come with this new, rapid-fire approach to dating, it does have some benefits. First of all, you are able to meet a large number of people in a short period of time. And let's face it: if all first dates lasted only eight minutes, the average life span of human beings would increase by ten years. Another good thing is that speed dating provides a safe, easy way to meet, greet, and reject a large number of potential relationships, and it's all done fairly anonymously. If

> **"**I've only been speed dating one time, but I thought it was so boring and repetitive. I kept thinking about that movie Thirteen Conversations About One Thing.**"**
>
> —Meridith

you do meet someone interesting, there's a chance that he'll put you down on his dating card as a match too, and you'll have a happy e-mail waiting for you in your in-box the next day. And as you know, it's always nice to get mail.

There are some ways, however, to avoid some of the problems mentioned earlier and to put the odds of meeting someone interesting in your favor:

- When it comes to speed dating, size does matter. You'll want to know how many people will be attending and what is the ratio of men to women.
- Got religion? If you know ahead of time that you have certain religious preferences, find an event that caters to your specific needs. They are out there. Also, if you would prefer to be in a crowd of people in similar professional lifestyles, look for events at higher-end restaurants. Speed dating can be a very overwhelming process and it's best to narrow the pool to find the particular fish you seek to catch.
- Most importantly, keep your sense of humor. The idea of meeting a dozen potential dates in an hour plays directly into the modern need of instant gratification. Meet, Match, Mate. The reality is that you will be lucky to meet one guy that you would like to talk to again. And that's a good outcome.

Used-Date Parties

I'd heard about Used-Date Parties for years and thought that the idea behind them was brilliant. Unfortunately I never got invited to one, nor did anyone else I knew. I figured that either Used-Date Parties were an urban legend or I wasn't hanging around with a cool enough circle of friends.

But then I saw Carrie Bradshaw and her two-dimensional friends go to a Used-Date Party on an episode of *Sex and the City,* and I knew that they really must exist. In case you've never heard of a Used-Date Party before, or don't watch *Sex and the City* (in which case you're probably suffering from a transgender problem), let me explain what it is. A Used-Date Party is a gathering like any other but when the invitation states BYOB, it doesn't mean to bring your own booze. It means to bring your old boyfriend. By doing so, the party is filled with available guys that other women have found worthy of dating. This idea takes the philosophy of recycling to a whole new level.

The first thing that you want to do when you're invited to a Used-Date Party is to decide which ex to bring along. If you have an ex who broke your heart, you may want to invite him just to show that you're over him (and, of course, to have him witness you flirt with a roomful of available men). Or maybe you want to take along a guy that you went out with a few times but have no interest in seeing again. You've dropped hints, but he's just not getting the message. Inviting him to a Used-Date Party is like dropping the atom bomb of hints.

Once you arrive at the party, it's a dating free for all. You know there's a roomful of available men and your adrenaline sets in. You feel like you're at a Barneys clearance sale and there's one Donna Karan blouse left in your size and a handful of grubby paws trying to grab it first. But Used-Date Parties are actually a bit more enjoyable because they usually have tasty snacks.

If you find a guy that interests you, chat with him awhile and ask him who he came with. Then, somewhere between your second wine spritzer and your fourth baby carrot, excuse yourself and track down the broad that brought him. You need to grill her like a burger on the Fourth of July to find out everything you can about your potential purchase. How long did they go out? Is he controlling? Did he cheat? Is he boring? Noncommittal? Or, like so many other fish in the sea, did she throw him back simply because he was too small? He must have some sort of problem and now is the time to find out exactly what it is. If his problem is merely superficial and can be fixed by proper etiquette and a good exfoliating loofa, rush right back before some other woman tries to get her grubby paws on him.

All in all, a Used-Date Party can be a very successful and enjoyable experience. The ratio of eligible bachelors is higher than at your average run of the mill party, you can meet these men in a casual, friendly environment, and of course, there are those tasty snacks. But that doesn't mean there aren't troubles in paradise. For just as there are a good proportion of available men, there are also a good proportion of available women. As you know, women are none too subtle when it comes to getting what they want. They pounce on their prey like a white tiger on Roy.

Another inherent flaw in this system is caused by an odd bit of human behavior: We don't want something until we see someone else wanting it. Anyone who's ever had a garage sale will recognize this strange form of human behavior. You'll see women have a tug-of-war over your old pair of parachute pants and suddenly, you're desperate to get them back. This same thing will happen when you witness your ex-boyfriend encircled by a group of bloodthirsty women. You'll experience newfound pangs of jealousy that you never thought existed. But when you get him back, you'll realize why you broke up with him in the first place and you'll have to break up with him all over again. Actually, you could just throw on those old parachute pants and he'll probably never call you again.

If you want to go to a Used-Date Party but aren't as cool as Carrie, Samantha, Charlotte, and Miranda, I have an idea for you. Simply log on to *www.greatboyfriends.com*. This Web site is chock-full of ex-lovers that are given the stamp of approval by their old girlfriends. It's quick and it's easy but unfortunately, there are no tasty snacks.

Get Your Fix

Starbucks has done more than introduce our culture to the joy of lattes and cappuccinos. They've also introduced millions of single people to their lovers and spouses. Because of all this matchmaking, coffeehouses have become more than just a place to get a caffeine boost. They've become a place to boost your love life as well.

When it comes to coffeehouses, not all are created equal. There are the artsy-fartsy types that tend to have nightly poetry readings and where an eclectic doodle on a napkin ends up framed on the wall. There are the ones that focus on entertainment and play live music every evening. And there are the ones that cater to a more upscale clientele that don't mind spending the equivalent of their monthly mortgage on their morning caffeine fix.

You'll find that most coffeehouses are chock-full of single guys. This is because men don't know how to cook and couldn't possibly perform the complex task of mixing hot water with coffee grounds. Therefore these dressed-up members of the working class are forced to go out for their coffee. Sure, it's a pain for them, but it gives you the opportunity to go out and pick up some "Joe" for yourself.

Coffeehouses can be wonderful places to meet someone. This is due to the following reasons:

- The lines to order your coffee tend to be long and the shops tend to be small, so you're forced to stand in close proximity with potential coffee-mates.
- Coffeehouses are crowded, so asking someone if you can share a table is a commonly accepted practice.
- Coffeehouses have a casual environment. They have comfortable chairs, cozy sofas, and soft lighting. They even have romantic, New-Agey music playing in the background. This makes them feel more like a living room than a store.
- Since most people frequent their local coffee shops each morning, you get to see the same faces day after day and are more comfortable making chitchat.
- Unlike at the gym, you're pretty much dolled up before stepping foot in a coffeehouse. You've had your morning shower, put on your office attire, and don't have sweat marks under your breasts.

One of the best things about meeting someone at a coffeehouse is that if you do hit it off and make a date to go out, you're going to feel much more comfortable with him than you would on most of your other first dates. That's because,

in a way, you've already had your first date. You sat around
for a while, had a cup of coffee, and listened to some music.
And you didn't even have to worry about what to wear or
that awkward good night kiss! So my advice to you is, if you
want to take a chance on love, wake up and smell the coffee.

Type of Insight You Can Get into a Guy's Character by Observing His Coffee-Ordering Habits

What He Does	What It Means
Plain black coffee	He's a purist. He likes vanilla ice cream and American cars, and he doesn't stray from the missionary position except on birthdays or after watching anything with Carmen Electra.
Half-cap vanilla	He's very high maintenance and anal-retentive.
Macchiato with 2 percent soy	He carries a lint brush with him at all times and is a stickler for good grammar. His perfect mate is Mary Poppins.
Leaves a big tip in the tip jar.	He's generous to a fault since 99.9 percent of the time the servers are unaware that a tip is even given, or if they are, they rarely acknowledge it.
Takes money out of the tip jar.	If you're into a guy that practices petty theft, this is the guy for you!
Insists on using that cardboard cup-holder sleeve.	He's a wimp with a low threshold for pain. He's the type of man who acts like he's dying whenever he gets a cold (actually, is there any other type of man?).
Loves those iced blended drinks.	He's in touch with his feminine side. He loves romantic comedies and screams if he ever sees a spider in the house.

Men's Hangouts

I think that the best place to find a man is to look for him in his natural habitat. It's there that a man is more relaxed and more himself and isn't focused on scoping the place for the deepest cleavage. If you've ever asked yourself, "Where are all the good men hiding?" then you should definitely visit one of these natural habitats.

In these sacred environments, women are anomalies, so the ratio of men to women is greatly in your favor. But be aware that these places are so macho that you may feel the sudden urge to pee standing up. So if you want to go on a manhunt, here are some jungles that you should venture into.

1. A Hardware Store
Now that TV is inundated with shows that teach home repair and maintenance, even the most stubborn couch potato is sliding off his spud and into a hardware store. He's learning how to do things around the house like fix a broken garbage disposal or build a wine rack made out of laundry lint. Because of this, men are always in need of a certain doohickey or a thingamabob that can only be found at their local hardware store.

Hardware stores are to men what beauty supply shops are to women. They both have an endless amount of aisles to browse through that are stocked with an endless amount of goodies. For women these goodies are styling products, face cream, and hair remover. For men they're needle nose pliers, socket wrenches, and table saws. In both cases, we can spend a long time checking out products that we never knew we needed until we saw them.

If you decide to venture into one of these musk-laden palaces, I suggest that you have a game plan. You should have a specific item you have in mind to buy. If you can't think of one, might I suggest a Microplane. I'm not quite sure what a Microplane was originally designed for, but it makes an excellent lemon zester and sells for a fraction of the price than the ones sold at those expensive kitchen supply stores.

Now that you have an item to shop for, browse the aisles for your desired item. No, not the Microplane; I'm talking about the guy. If you see one that interests you, all you have to do is ask him if he knows where they keep the Microplanes. Hopefully this guy won't think you're a "nut" and won't "bolt" or "screw" you over (sorry, I can be quite punny).

I hope that you'll find the man of your dreams at a hardware store. But even if you don't meet anyone, try not to be sad. Instead of feeling that life just gave you lemons, now with your new Microplane, you can make your own zesty lemonade!

2. Any Place Affiliated with Golf

I don't know what it is about the game of golf that's so alluring to men. Is it their innate instinct to hold a club? Their obsession with lawn care? Or their continual desire to put something in a hole? Whatever the reason, men are as attracted to golf as women are to shoes. Because of this, men are also attracted to all places that deal with golf and golf products.

If you want to take advantage of this male obsession and become an obsession of a male yourself, you'll want to hang out at golf places. This not only means golf courses but driving ranges, putting greens, and golf pro shops as well.

And don't worry if you don't know how to play the game. I'm sure that there are many golf "experts" who will jump at the chance to teach you the perfect swing. There's nothing more erotic to a man than nuzzling up behind a woman and teaching her where to hold her hands on his staff. It's a very sensual experience for him and puts the "fore" in foreplay.

3. Sports Bars

As we all know, sports bars are a favorite hangout for men. That's because of their inherent genius of combining two of men's greatest passions: sports and bars. There is no such equivalent hangout for women. I image if they ever had a place we could go for a massage while being spoon-fed cookie dough, it would come pretty darn close.

To a man, a sports bar is about as near to heaven as he can get on Earth. Where else is it acceptable behavior for a guy to drink, scream, cuss, and belch in public? Because of this, sports bars are busier than a one-armed paper hanger or a cranberry merchant in November.

Although these places are filled with men, don't be intimidated to enter (although the beer stench may be enough to intimidate anyone). Women are not just welcome in sports bars; they are encouraged to be there. They're good patrons, they buy a lot of T-shirts and souvenirs, and the men need something else to look at during commercial breaks when there's not a beer ad playing.

I know what you're saying: "But I don't know the rules of the games." Luckily, that's not a problem. All you need to know is to cheer whenever a guy you like cheers. Men are incredibly loyal to their specific team and if you root for the opponent, this man will never be loyal to you.

The Silver Lining

I know that the vast amount of times that you flirt with a man, it doesn't end up with the two of you going on a date, but that doesn't mean that the time spent together has to be a waste. In fact, there's something you can learn from every man that you meet, if you just know what to ask. For instance:

1. If you're picked up by a doctor, make sure he teaches you the difference between a viral infection and a bacterial one so that you know if you'll need antibiotics for future illnesses.
2. If you're chatting with a policeman, make sure to uncover the secret way to get out of a ticket in case you're ever pulled over.
3. If a chef sits next to you, be sure to ask him how to make a good roux . . . the basis for all good sauces.
4. If you're flirting with someone who works retail, try to stick it out until after the holiday season so you can take full advantage of his employee discount.
5. If you're at a bar with a handyman, be sure to find out what to do when your garbage disposal breaks and you've already tried the reset button trick.
6. If you're sitting next to someone who works for the telephone company, ask him how you can get around all those frustrating computer operators and actually speak directly to a person. And then be sure to pass that secret on to me.

chapter four

let the games begin

If you have trouble remembering rules like "i before e except after c" and "two quarts equal one gallon," then you're going to have a tough time remembering the rules of dating. That's because there are so many different rules to choose from and they're constantly changing depending on your age, your circumstances, and what Dr. Laura book you're reading. For instance, if you meet a guy who tickles your fancy and he asks you if you're dating anyone, what do you tell him? If you tell him that you're not, he'll presume that you don't have what it takes to keep a man. If you tell him that you're not seeing anyone special, then he'll assume that you're dating a bunch of guys and that you're a slut. So what's a girl to do?

As you can see, when it comes to love, there needs to be an official rule book to follow. I know, I know, you don't want to play any games. You want to go up to any guy that interests you, ask him for his number, and invite him out to dinner. Then on the date, you want to feel free to discuss any topic that pops into your head, like your desperate need to get married or your latest outbreak of herpes. If this is the way you want to find a mate, fine, go right ahead. But I predict that he'll dump you as easily as last night's dinner.

I understand how you feel. I went through that au naturel way of dating myself. I thought that playing games seemed artificial and that I was above all of that. But if you think about it, playing games of courtship is actually a very natural thing. In fact, almost every member of the animal kingdom follows some type of mating ritual. The cricket rubs his hind legs together to serenade his little love bug. The lobster pees on his beloved in hopes of attracting her. And we all know about the black widow that seduces her lover and then proceeds to bite his head off. So you see, our ritual of flipping our hair and batting a few eyelashes doesn't seem so bad after all.

Now that we all agree that playing a few games isn't the worst thing in life, we have to agree on one more thing: that you're not going to learn how to play any of them from me. When it comes to playing the game of love, I still consider myself to be a rookie. Even though I've been wearing my team jersey for more than two decades, I'm still perplexed at how to score and find myself making an awful lot of foul plays. But the one thing that I have learned is that if you find a set of rules that works well for you, then by all means, put on your kneepads and get into the game.

But even though I'm not going to preach to you about trivial details like when to accept a date for a Saturday night, and how often to make eye contact with a man that interests you, I am going to share some broad dating theories that seem to make an awful lot of sense.

Location, Location, Location

The first rule of thumb is where not to find a guy. In fact, this cardinal rule is the same one that applies to real estate. It's all about location, location, location. What I mean by this is that you should exercise extreme caution when going out with a man who is a part of your routine existence. Get out your number two pencils, girls, and figure out if this new relationship is worth taking the risk. Before you proceed, you need to weigh the pros and cons to see if dating him is worth the time and trouble you'd have to go through to replace him with someone of equal or greater value. And you thought high school math would never come in handy when you grew up!

Some examples of men that are not geographically desirable are your cute hairdresser who squeezes you in even on his busiest day, the flirty waiter that always gives you a seat by the window, the salesman at your favorite clothing store that puts new items aside for you before they sell out, and of course, every man that lives within a one-mile radius of your domicile, who you could easily run into.

I know this rule of location, location, location seems obvious, and we're all aware of the rule that we shouldn't schitzu where we eat-zu, but I can't tell you how many times these rules are conveniently forgotten whenever a set of cute dimples comes our way. Believe me girls, I know from where I speak, for I myself have broken this sacred rule of dating once before.

I used to have this amazing car mechanic. He could tune an engine like Stradivarius could tune a violin. This automotive genius would make my old klunker purr like a kitten, and one day when he saw me in my workout attire, he wanted to do the same thing to me. I heard that little voice inside my head say, "Don't do it. Dating your car mechanic is not a good idea." But I stuffed a gag in her itty-bitty mouth and went out with him anyway.

As it turned out, my inner voice was right. I ended up having a horrible time. I followed this guy to a little, out of the way restaurant where he proceeded to tell me over and over again where he'd like to put his dipstick. Halfway through the meal I got up and left, not knowing where the hell I was. Not only did I have to find my way home, I also had to find a new car mechanic. To this day my inner voice has never forgiven me, and my car has never driven the same.

So learn from my mistakes. Do the math and weigh the pros and cons before you accept a date from someone in your hood, or someone that fixes what's underneath it. If numbers are not your strong suit, just listen to your own inner voice and be sure not to piss her off. Mine is still giving me the silent treatment, which is why I've worn several embarrassing outfits in public, and told a few dear friends that yes, their butts did indeed look fat in those pants.

Dating Within Our League

When it comes to playing the game of love, we're all in a different league. There's the pee-wee league, the minors, and of course, the one that's reserved for only the best-looking players, the major leagues. Even though we're not given our ranking along with our birth certificate and those free samples of formula when we're born, we're all fully aware what league we play in. No dating etiquette book has ever contained a rule that we must play within our own league, but it's as well known as "stop on red; go on green."

But if we're lucky, once in a lifetime when the angels play their harps and the leprechauns find a four-leaf clover, the rules can change. For me that day happened when I turned twenty-three. That's when I met the most gorgeous man that I've ever seen in real life. He had rugged features and a great physique, and best of all, he had an interest in me! I couldn't believe my good luck and kept expecting a host to reveal himself and show me where the camera was hidden! I came to realize that this guy actually liked me! I figured that God was trying to make it up to me for making me need braces.

Once we finished making small talk, none of which I can remember for the life of me because of my semiconscious state of mind, my dreamboat asked me out. I managed to stammer out a "yes" along with a long sliver of drool and a few facial tics, and off we went. As we walked into the restaurant, I felt like I was deserting my team. I had moved up to the big leagues and oh, how wonderful it felt. All the women in the place were looking at me, then looking at him, and then at me.

One of the good things about going out with a gorgeous man is that you get the most amazing service. The waitress kept coming over to our table to see if we needed anything and she even gave us a free dessert. I swear if there really is such a thing as reincarnation, I want to come back as a good-looking man. Easy dates and free dessert. What more could anyone want?

As the evening went on, I had a hard time focusing on the conversation. My mind kept wandering, as I pondered what ulterior motives he could have for going out with me.

Was he trying to make another woman jealous? Did he think I came from money? Had he heard somewhere that women with perfectly straight teeth give better oral sex? The whole date was quite unnerving. In the end, we only went out one more time and then parted ways. Who was I kidding anyway? You can't go breaking this unwritten rule about not dating outside of your league, and besides, how was I ever supposed to truly relax around a guy that looked better in a pair of jeans than I did?

If you're ever lucky enough to go against the rules and date someone outside of your league, you should enjoy it while it lasts. Savor every second, because this abnormality of nature tends to have a lifespan as short as a tsetse fly. If you've never had the good fortune to stray from your team, I have one tidbit of advice to offer about the male psyche that may help you achieve this goal, and it's called "playing hard to get." Read on.

Single Fellas in the Mist

I was always perplexed by the rule of playing hard to get. If a guy I met ignored me and showed absolutely no interest whatsoever, the last thing I would ever do is pursue him. My ego is frail enough, thank you very much, and I know that seeking out even more rejection would crush it faster than an elephant's ass on a house of cards. But that's where men seem to differ from women. Well, in that and the fact that they never feel the urge to clean up before the cleaning lady comes over.

Because of my outgoing nature and my inability to attract men, I find that I've become friends with a lot of guys. This not only saves me money by not having to buy Gyno-gel, but it's allowed me access into a world that I would never have been privy to otherwise. I'm like a young Dian Fossey, but instead of studying the mysterious behavior of gorillas, I study the mysterious behavior of single men.

Because of my unique position, I've learned that the "rule" of playing hard to get, as silly as it is, does have some merit. I've witnessed time and time again how my male friends would obsess over women who showed them as much interest as last year's fashions. In fact, it seemed that the more these women rejected their advances, the more these men became attracted to them. I know one man who actually bought a house just because a woman he was obsessed with said that she liked it. He had hoped that she would be so impressed by him that she'd fall madly in love despite the fact she had put out a restraining order against him. From my observations, I deduced that the intensity with which a man likes a woman who is disinterested in him is in direct proportion to how much heartache this woman will inflict upon him.

Even though I don't know why men demonstrate this odd behavior, I do know that plenty of insightful women understand this abnormality and use it to their advantage. They've had plenty of success getting a man's attention by simply ignoring him. I, too, learned this valuable tidbit of information, not because I ignored a man's advances, but because I made the horrible mistake of pursuing a man who showed interest in me.

It happened years ago but the memory is as clear as if it happened yesterday. I was at a party and talked with a gorgeous man who turned my legs into jelly. But when he was about to leave without getting my number, I knew it was up to me to make the first move. I somehow mustered up the same courage a bungee jumper needs before taking the plunge. But unfortunately I fell flat on my head, because when I asked this guy out, he said "no." His rejection was so traumatic that here it is years later, and just thinking about it makes me nauseous. Actually, that may have more to do with the fact I just ate a box of Snow Caps, but nonetheless, I still find it very upsetting.

So if you want to take advantage of a guy's warped need to be ignored, go right ahead. I think you'll have far better luck getting a guy's attention simply by giving him none of yours. But if you still want to make the first move and think that this neurosis in men can be overcome, go ahead and give it a try. While you're at it, you may want to try to defy gravity as well, for I'm sure that you'll have the same success with challenging that force of nature.

Pick-Up Lines

Now that you've learned a little bit about the male psyche, let me fill you in on one aspect of male stupidity. One of the silliest yet universal "rules" of dating is that you are required to hear men attempt to impress you by uttering ridiculous phrases. These phrases are more commonly known as "pick-up lines," and men have been using them since the beginning of time. In fact, it's very well documented that the first pick-up line ever to be uttered was used by Adam when he saw Eve frolicking in the garden. He turned to her and said, "This isn't an asp under my fig leaf; I'm just glad to see ya!"

I wish I could tell you that pick-up lines have evolved since biblical days, but alas, they have not. They remain barbaric, insulting, and just plain idiotic, and you still remain their victim. If you have yet to hear your first pick-up line, rest assured that at some point during your dating career, you will. In case you don't know what to look out for, they will sound something like this:

1. Is that Windex you're wearing, because I can see myself in your pants.
2. Your body's name must be Visa, because it's everywhere I wanna be.
3. I may not be Fred Flintstone but I bet I can make your Bed Rock.
4. Just call me milk, because I'll do your body good.
5. Do you want to play house? You be the screen door and I'll slam you all night long.
6. If your left leg was Thanksgiving and your right leg was Christmas, could I visit you between the holidays?
7. Can I buy you a drink or do you just want the money?
8. I may not be the best-looking guy here, but I'm the only one talking to you.

I can only assume that the reason that these phrases have survived for so long is that men must have enough success using them to continue to do so. Sure, it can't be more than one out of every million women, but it's just enough encouragement to keep these lines alive and well.

My advice is that if you're as offended by these stupid remarks as I am, don't give the jerkwads who say them any positive reinforcement. Maybe if these lines are ignored by 100 percent of the female population, they'll vanish over the next few generations along with our appendix and pinky toe.

How to Read a Man's Body

It's a fact: People lie. If you don't believe me, just take a look at the weight on your driver's license. But when it comes to lying, it's the men who are the experts in the field. They lie about their income. They lie about the size of their penis. And they lie when it comes to saying the three words that every woman longs to hear from a desirable man: "I'll call you." But then when you never hear from the guy, you realize that you've been duped. You wonder how your instincts could have been so wrong. Here you thought that you had great chemistry with him and didn't realize that he had more interest in his gin and tonic.

I know that many a book has been written about what to do if a guy never calls, but I'd like to show you a trick to avoid waiting by the phone in the first place. First of all, when this happens, don't be so hard on yourself. It's not your fault. Men are in fact quite talented liars and can deliver the line "You have beautiful eyes" with the same theatrical mastering Tom Cruise did when saying "You complete me." Secondly, that doesn't mean that you have to be a victim of their deception. You just need to know what to look out for. You can outsmart a lying man if you know how to speak his language. Body language, that is. I'm going to fill you in on some secret behaviors that a man will display if he's genuinely interested in you or if he's just a liar, liar, pants on fire:

1. Is this man exhibiting good posture or is he slouching? In general, if a guy's bored, he'll tend to slouch. If he sits up or even leans forward toward you, that's a good sign that he's interested in you.

2. When you talk, does he appear interested in what you're saying? Does he nod his head from time to time as you speak, or is he just nodding off?

3. Try to notice if the man you're with mimics your behavior. Does he shift his weight in his seat if you do? Does he breath in the same rhythm as you do? These are a couple of unconscious signs that he's enjoying your company.

4. Are his arms open or are they crossed in front of him? If his arms are crossed, it could mean that he's putting up a wall between the two of you. That, or he's just cold.

5. Be aware of the moment that he says that he'll call. Did the pitch in his voice change? Did he say "um" or "ah" a lot when he spoke? Did he look away when he told you he'd call you? Did his hand cover any part of his face, especially his mouth, while he was talking? If the answer to any of these questions is yes, he may be a liar.

6. Do his feet or legs move around nervously? This is a sign that he may not be being truthful. Of course, it could also mean that he has an urgent desire to pee.

It's an unfortunate truth, but all men are just giant Pinocchios walking around with stiff wooden protrusions. Because of this, we women have to learn an entirely new language so that we can really hear what a man is trying to tell us, and not just what we want to hear.

When the F*** Will He Call?

Now that you know where not to meet a man, what stupid lines he'll use to woo you, and what his body language is saying, now you need some insight as to when you can expect a guy to call. The truth is that women have searched for the answer to this burning question for as long as historians have searched for the Holy Grail. We seem to think that there is a certain formula that men use in determining when they will make that all-important call. We calculate hypotheses and examine theorems in hopes of better understanding this theory of relativity for romance. The closest answer that we've come up with for how long it takes a man to call is determined by taking the day of the week that you met, multiplying it by how many other numbers he collected that evening, and dividing that sum by your bra size.

One thing you need to understand about dating is that guys have their own version of the dating rule book, although theirs is covered with pizza sauce and beer stains. They have their own guidelines when it comes to determining how much time can pass from when they got your phone number to when they place that call without running the risk of appearing too anxious or being forgotten. Understandably, you may be concerned that if you don't hear from him right away, you never will. You can rationalize the wait by assuming he's either lost your number or has been hit by a truck and is lying in an unconscious state, desperate to move his comatose finger so that he can call you.

Even though most rule books will tell you that a guy will wait approximately 2.5 days to call, I can provide you with a lot more insight so that you can pinpoint the exact time that he'll call:

1. What big games are on TV? Actually, that's a silly question, because the way guys see it, all games are big games. But if the guy that you gave your number to is

into football, you'll have to wait until the game is over before he picks up the phone. Knowing that there is a game on Monday night, Thursday night, and that there are games on all day Saturday and Sunday, you may have to wait until after Super Bowl Sunday to get a call.

2. What time of day is it? A lot of guys will call you at night, sometime after dinner but before it's time for bed. They know that if they call you any earlier, you'll be busy making dinner and they know how grumpy a woman can get when she's hungry. They also know that if they call too late in the evening, they may wake you up and start things off on the wrong foot. Sometime between eight and ten at night, a guy knows that your blood sugar will be at a stable level and that you'll be in a relaxed state of mind.

3. What does the big hand on the clock say? You may also notice that guys tend not to call on the hour or half-hour. They don't want you to think that they're just sitting around watching TV and calling during a commercial break. They want to appear that they have other, more important things to do. Of course, the only important thing on their agenda is cutting their toenails, but they don't want you to know that.

4. What day of the week is it? As if a guy's brain can handle any more thinking, he also has to decide what day of the week to call you. This problem can be quite difficult because they have to take into account a couple of factors: when they met you and on what day of the week they want to see you. For instance, if a guy meets you on a Tuesday, and he has tickets for a Sunday concert, he'll probably give you a call on Thursday night. Sounds easy, but things can get a lot trickier. For example if you meet on a Thursday and he wants to see you on Saturday,

when should he call? If you've answered "he shouldn't,"
then you now think like a man and you are awarded your
honorary set of testicles.

The reason that a guy shouldn't call is that his only day
to call would be on Friday and that would make him appear
much too desperate. Besides, a guy knows that he can't possibly call you on Friday since you wouldn't answer the phone
anyway, because you want him to think that you're out and
not just home organizing your utensil drawer. You're playing by the rules, too, remember?

I know that it's frustrating just sitting around waiting
for the phone to ring, but as you can see, a lot of thought,
time, and logic goes into a guy placing that all-important
first phone call. So let this guy put a little mental work into
this call. It may be the most amount of thought that he'll
put into your relationship until he's done something really
bad that he needs to be forgiven for.

Being Stood Up

Once a guy does call, there's another biggie that I want to fill
you in on. Another unwritten "rule" is that at some point in
your dating career, you will be stood up. If you haven't been
yet, just wait. It's as inevitable as death, taxes, and someone walking into the room after you farted. There are many
memorable moments in life, like the first time you went to
Disneyland, the first time you took your driving test, and
the first time you saw Janet Jackson reveal her breast at the
Super Bowl. And of course, you can never forget the first
time that you were stood up on a date.

The term "stood up" can mean several different things. For when it comes right down to it, there are actually three different and distinct degrees of this type of abuse.

1. The first degree is when a guy asks you out for Friday night but you never hear from him again. He doesn't call during the week to confirm the date or even to decide on a place to meet. In this case you make plans to go out to dinner with a friend and decide never to talk to him again.

2. The second degree is when a guy asks you out for Friday night and does call you to confirm. The problem arises when he never comes by to pick you up. You've wasted all this time and effort getting ready for a date that never shows. In this case, you take yourself to the movies and decide never to talk to him again.

3. The third degree is when he asks you out for Friday and you agree to meet him at a certain restaurant at a designated time. You get there on time, order a glass of Merlot, and wait for him to arrive. About halfway through your drink he's still not there and you start to worry that something's happened to him. You check your cell phone. It's working. You call your home machine. No messages. The waiter comes by and asks if you'd like to order, but you decline and tell him that you'll wait a bit longer.

   By now your worry has turned into rage. You feel uncomfortable sitting alone, and you curse this guy and think that he better have one damned good excuse for being late. You finish your drink and make a pact that if he doesn't arrive in five more minutes with a blood-soaked bandage wrapped around his head, you're out of there. But then the realization hits you like a ton of bricks: You've been stood up! In this case you order another glass of wine, order the most comforting thing on the menu, decide never to see him again, and of course, make the decision to become a lesbian.

Sure, maybe he had a good excuse. Maybe his car broke down and his cell phone had a dead battery and all the pay phones in the city were broken. It could happen. Or maybe he took one look at you and bolted! Or at least that's what you're thinking. If he calls apologetically, go ahead and give him a second chance if you wish, but I wouldn't dream of it. I think that the most insulting thing a guy could do is stand a woman up. Face it, people do what they want to do, and if he knew that he had a date with $1 million cash that Friday night, there's not a chance in hell he'd leave it sitting alone at a restaurant drinking a glass of Merlot.

But the most important lesson learned is that, even if you are stood up, you can still enjoy the pleasure of your own company. Movies are still entertaining, food still tastes delicious, and wine is just as soothing. In most cases, being by yourself is far better than being on a date. Just check out this next rule and you'll see what I mean.

The Stepford Date

Here you are on a date after spending hours putting yourself together. You're wearing a wonderful outfit, your hair is coifed to perfection, and your new bra is lifting and separating you like it was Moses and your boobs were the Red Sea. You think that you look fabulous. But at some point in the

❝ I went out with this guy once and was instantly turned off by the way he smelled. When I left the restaurant, it still smelled bad, and I realized that I stepped in dog poop on the way to the restaurant. The guy never called because he must have thought that poop was my normal smell. **❞**

—Ilyse

evening you excuse yourself and go to the ladies room only to find that you have a booger the size of a corn nut dangling from your nose.

You're devastated! Here you thought the reason your date had trouble looking into your eyes was because he was so taken by your beauty, when all along it was because your face made him want to puke. Little did you know that looking at you was like witnessing a live birth coming out of your nostril!

After such a catastrophic experience, you're paralyzed with anxiety. It seems that you've broken the most fundamental "rule" of the first date: you must appear perfect. Everyone knows that on date number one you are forbidden to have any bodily functions whatsoever. You cannot show any flaws. You cannot spit when you talk. You cannot belch after a hearty meal. You cannot emit any body odor of any kind. The truth is that in order to have a successful first date, it's imperative that you become a Stepford date.

Men are a predictable species and women can predict that they will reject us for a vast array of superficial reasons. We've seen enough *Seinfeld* reruns to know this to be a fact.

We've seen Jerry dump the woman with "man-hands" and the "low-talker" who speaks so quietly that only a dog can hear her. We're familiar with the girl he tossed aside simply because she kept rash cream in her medicine cabinet and the one that had the nerve to assign him too high of a number on her speed dial. And it's not just Jerry that acts in this irrational manner. In fact, the reason that this show was so successful was that men finally found a television character that they could relate to.

Take my friend Steve, for instance. He dumped a girlfriend once, based solely on the fact that one of her ears was noticeably larger than the other. And my pal Jon rejected one simply because he thought the webbing between her fingers was too prominent. I also know for a fact that a certain celebrity insists that his girlfriend use a separate bathroom than he does because he knows that he'd have to break up with her if he were to ever smell her doodie.

Sure, on some level men know that women are only human, but I find that they don't actually want to see any hint of this human quality for quite some time after they've been together, if ever at all. They want to put their goddess on a pedestal where they can look up to her, admire her beauty, and easily peek under her dress.

Just so there's no confusion, I'm going to lay out some of the cardinal no-no's of what not to do on a first date. In fact, most of these no-no's shouldn't be committed until after your relationship has developed a strong foundation, or there's a multicarat ring placed on your finger. Here are a few of the first-date disasters that you'll want to avoid committing:

1. Do not pass gas or smell stinky in any way.
2. Do not have crust in the corner of your eyes.

3. Do not have hair sticking out of any of your moles. In fact, it's a good idea not to have any moles at all.
4. Do not have pasty white buildup in the corners of your mouth.
5. Do not expose your foot if your second toe is longer than your big one.
6. Do not have any enlarged pores.
7. Do not sneeze in a short consecutive manner like a toy poodle.
8. Do not have any sweat stains under your arms. In fact, it's best to abstain from sweating entirely.
9. Do not have bad breath (see rule #1).

In case you're not sure of whether a certain behavior is acceptable or a no-no, it's best to abstain from doing it. As you know, it's better to be safe than be single.

Zip That Lip!

One of the reasons that dating truly sucks is that you can't always say what's on your mind. Well, you can, but because men are of such a fearful breed, even the subtlest hint about a certain topic can make them panic as much as you do if your period is late. Don't get me wrong. I'm not saying that you can't ever talk about certain subjects. In fact, I encourage honesty and feel that communication is a vital part of keeping a relationship healthy and strong. I just advise that you wait to discuss certain delicate topics until sometime after you've consummated your wedding vows.

I don't want you to think I'm sexist, either. We women aren't the only ones who censor our first date conversation.

Men have their own subjects to avoid, like if they have a certain fetish for women's underwear, the fact that they still live at home with their mommy, or the troubles they have due to their small penis. Both men and women agree that a new relationship is a very fragile thing and that certain topics of conversation would cause it to crumble like Justine Bateman's career.

Most of the topics that you should avoid are fairly obvious. But in case you're a novice at dating, you've had a recent lobotomy, or your own inner voice is pissed off at you for something that you did, here is a list I've compiled of some of these topics of conversation that you should keep hush-hush about if you don't want to make your fearful man fear for his life:

1. Anything that has to do with your desire to get married.
2. Anything that has to do with your menstrual cycle or feminine hygiene products of any kind.
3. Anything that has to do with your strong desire to have children, including how many you want, what you want to name them, or that computerized photo you had made of what they might look like.
4. Anything that has to do with politics. (This is always a heated topic, so it should be avoided until there is more heat between you.)
5. Anything that has to do with a medical condition like irritable bowel syndrome.
6. Anything that has to do with your past or present therapy sessions or any mood-stabilizing medications that you're required to take.
7. Anything that has to do with your huge credit card debt.

8. Anything that has to do with your aversion to giving blow-jobs or any other commonly requested sexual activity.

Of course, if you don't want to waste any time dating a man that won't stick around, go right ahead and spill the beans. But I've found when it comes to discussing certain subjects, mum is indeed the word. If you ever slip and find yourself getting into any of these off-limit topics, quickly find a way to change the conversation to auto racing, strip clubs, or the WWF. Maybe you can counteract any damage you may have caused by inducing a quick shot of testosterone.

The Art of Rejection

Up until now we've only been focusing on the rules of how you can get a man. But there is another aspect to dating that can be just as challenging and there seems to be no written rules about this subject: How to get a guy who's interested in you to stop being so interested. It's surprising that when you like someone who doesn't like you back, it's incredibly painful. But when a guy likes you and you don't like him, it's incredibly annoying.

We've all been there. Either we meet someone that we're not interested in right off the bat and he asks for our number, or we go out with someone, have a horrible time, and he asks if he can see us again. In both of these situations, we're faced with the challenge of having to reject someone, and that challenge is never an easy one. To make matters worse, guys aren't as sensitive as women are, so they

don't understand the subtle hints that are thrown their way.
Because of this, we've had to rely on lies and manipulation
in order to get what we want. It's funny that the reasons that
men find women so difficult are the very same things that
they've inspired us to become.

If you've been chatting with someone at a bar or party
who asks for your number but you have no desire to pursue
a relationship with him, here are a couple of suggestions on
how to handle the situation:

1. If a man asks for you or number and you don't want him
   to have it, give him a number that's one digit off. This
   way, it flows easily from your mouth and he won't know
   that you're lying. Occasionally you'll meet a man who's
   been through this before and will systematically go
   through all the digits until he gets the number right. It
   seems that men are like that new strain of bacteria that's
   evolved to be immune to antibiotics.

2. If this doesn't appeal to you, go to *www.rejectionhotline.
   com* before you go out for the evening. There, you'll be

> **❝**I gave my number to a guy because I didn't have the
> courage not to. When he called I tried to let him down gently
> but he never got the message. Finally, I had my assistant tell
> him point blank that I had no interest in dating him. She felt
> so sorry for the guy that she ended up going out with him
> instead, and they actually went out for five months.**❞**
>
> —Amy

given a phone number to carry and give out to the losers you may meet. When he calls that number, he'll hear a prerecorded message that will reject him in a humorous yet not so subtle manner. This site has become so popular that they get over 1 million calls per month from over thirty cities. If that's not proof that dating sucks, I don't know what is!

But if you don't feel comfortable following either of those suggestions, go ahead and give the guy your number. But realize that when you do, that the chances of him calling you are high. When he does call, here are a couple of suggestions for what to do:

1. If you do give a guy your phone number, it's best to screen your calls for a few days and if he leaves a message, don't return it. You hope that by doing this, he'll get the message that you're not interested. Unfortunately, as it turns out, most men are denser than a holiday fruitcake.

2. If that doesn't work, you have to take his call. When he asks you out, make up some excuse. Tell him that you're on your way out to pick up your herpes medication and that you'll call him back. Of course, don't ever call him back. Although oftentimes the guy will get the hint, in some cases he'll still give you another call. I don't know if it's because they're really that dense or if they're too scared of rejection. Personally, I'd go with the dense thing.

3. If the subtle approach doesn't seem to be working, be tougher. Tell him that your old boyfriend just called and you're going to give it another chance. Tell him that you're just not ready to start dating and that you'll give

him a call when you are. Or tell him that you've realized
that you're a lesbian. Sure, he'll still feel rejected, but the
visuals it provides may just make it worth it.
4. If none of these approaches work, you have no other
choice but to be honest. Tell him that you just don't feel
any chemistry with him. But be sure to be as nice as you
can when you say it. Rejecting a guy is a delicate balance
of making sure that they get the hint while not turning
him into a stalker.

I know what you're saying. Why can't you just be direct
with the guy upfront? If you tell him right from the start
that you're not interested, you can save yourself a lot of aggra-
vation down the road. The reason that we don't is because
we've become so good at using lies and manipulation, that
it's become second nature to us, like breathing or putting on
mascara while we drive.

When Should You Sleep with Him?

Out of all the rules that the dating books preach, none is
as clear-cut as those that dictate when you should have sex
with a man for the first time. Many books tell you that if you
have sex too soon, you run the risk of the guy losing interest and never calling you again. They say if you have it too
late, the guy will get frustrated and move along to someone
who's an easier lay. I'm not a true believer in following any
rules, which is why I occasionally run with scissors.
  Because of this, I'm not going to advise you either way.
Everyone has their own beliefs and ethics that they follow,
and you're a big girl now and can decide what's right for

you. But I will say that these rules were created for a reason, and that reason is that having sex does change the relationship. At least for us women. Once we've shared our body with a man, we feel closer to him than before we did the deed. We tend to become more clingy and needy and even more demanding. Men, on the other hand, leave their emotional feelings on the floor next to the bed, along with their socks and dirty pair of Hanes.

When it comes to deciding when to have sex for the first time, just make sure that it's the right time for you. Don't do it because he bought you a twelve-course meal and you feel like you owe him something in return. Don't do it because he's called you a tease and you want to prove him wrong. Deciding to sleep with someone is a big decision and you can't just undo it like a politician does a campaign promise.

Besides, you have one big advantage that men don't have. Men are easy to seduce. Because of this, you don't have to rush to a decision. You know that at a drop of a hat, he'll give you the thumbs up (as well as another part of his anatomy). Men, however, have a much harder time trying to get a woman in bed. A man has to spend hours wining and dining a woman and saying all the right things at all the right times. And even if he does get her in the mood, that mood can instantly turn sour after he looks longingly at her and says, "Hey, I didn't know a woman could grow a mustache!"

So if you're thinking of having sex for any reason other than it's the right time for you, STOP! Realize that when you're ready to put yourself out there, he'll be ready to be the one to put himself in you. And most important, if you do have sex with a man and he never calls you again, don't despair. You should consider yourself lucky for sparing yourself all that future heartache after falling for a guy who's a loser. After all, he's lost out on the best thing that could have happened to him.

Don't Be Such a Girl

How many times has it happened that you've gone out with a wonderful man and clicked like you've never clicked before? You look at him and see your entire future in his eyes. You envision a wedding cake, a three-bedroom house, and a bedside drawer full of fun sex toys. You feel a connection that's deep and profound and you're sure that this guy is the one that you've been looking for. But then, surprise, surprise, you never hear from him again! Or, maybe you do hear from him, but only once or twice a month, just enough to make you mad. Or maybe you decide to sleep with him, have the best sex of your life, and then he text messages you twelve days later with the tender message of, "Hey babe, how's it hangin'?"

Sure, this guy tells you that he's into you, and you have an incredible time whenever you're together, but then he kisses you goodbye without mentioning a word of when you'll ever see him again. You tell yourself that he's sincere but that he must be really busy at work or that he's got to help some friends move or any one of a hundred other excuses to rationalize why he's not making you a priority. But the sad truth is that if you have to rationalize his feelings toward you, then he just doesn't care about you the way that you'd like him to.

The reason for this is that men are simple creatures. The only thing that rattles around in their empty little heads is a long list of football stats and a mental picture of Jennifer

Lopez in that green gown she was on the brink of falling out of at the Grammys. The fact of the matter is that when a guy wants to do something, there's not a hell of a lot of things that can stand in his way. If he wants to see you on the weekend, he's going to call you early in the week to lock you in. But if he doesn't care that much, you'll get a call about an hour before the movie starts, after all the girls that he really likes told him that they had plans. And instead of being upset, you're like every other typical girl and feel grateful just to be called. That, my friend, is why love stinks.

But all of that pain and frustration can be avoided if you simply know what to look out for. If you meet a guy that you like and he tells you that he'll call you the next day but instead calls you two days later, don't be happy that he called you at all. Instead, fight your instinct to be flattered that he went to all the trouble of picking up a phone and dialing your number. Stop being so self-destructive as to believe that the reason he didn't call you when he said that he would is because he's playing hard to get. You need to open your eyes, be kind to yourself, and really listen to what he's saying. He's telling you that he's not a dependable guy. He's telling you that he doesn't think you're special, because he was off doing something else that he enjoyed more than talking to you. And he's telling you that he doesn't think enough of you to stop you from waiting by the phone for a call that will never come.

You may ask yourself why a guy can't just be honest and tell you the truth in the first place. Why does he have to lie when he knows full well that he isn't going to call? The reason is that a guy's highest priority is to avoid confrontation with a woman at all cost. They know how angry we can get if we're hurt and how much we like to seek revenge. They've seen *Fatal Attraction*. Because of this, a guy would much rather string a woman along than cut her loose. Besides, he never knows when he might need to make a booty call and you may just come in handy.

What I want to get through that beautiful head of yours is that if a guy says that he has an early meeting, or that he has to go home to feed his cat, or any other excuse not to spend time with you, he's not doing it for any other reason than you're not that important to him. If you were, you would know it and you wouldn't have to make any excuses or rationalizations. Know in your heart that you deserve someone better who will step up to the plate and make you a priority.

I know it hurts, but when it comes right down to it, you really can't hate him for feeling this way. Well, okay, if it makes you feel any better, go right ahead. I'm sure that you've been out with many a guy who thought that you were the cat's meow when all you thought was that he was a nasty hairball. And now that the tables have turned, do yourself a big favor and let him go. If you don't, you're in for years of heartache and frustration trying to get a man to feel a certain way toward you that he just isn't capable of feeling. Listen to your heart and to Bonnie Raitt, and know that you can't make him love you if he won't.

Nice Guys Finish Last

Some rules are much easier said than followed. Need to lose weight? Eat less food. Have credit card debt? Stop spending money. Want to get married? Find a nice guy and settle down. But when it comes to finding a great guy, sometimes you can be your own worst enemy. After each heartbreak, you whine and complain about how your boyfriend has done you wrong. You agonize over why you can't ever meet a guy who treats you the way you deserve to be treated. One that will love you, respect you, and say "God bless you" when you sneeze. And then suddenly it happens. Out of nowhere, a guy just like this happens to appear. One that calls you when he says he's going to call. One that offers you his jacket whenever you feel cold. One that has a steady job and a retirement plan. And one that does what no other man before him has ever done: put the toilet seat down.

But when you meet a nice guy, do you embrace him with open arms and register for overpriced kitchen appliances? No. More often than not, you toss him away as if he were that expensive jar of cream that promised to make your chest bigger. You tell yourself that this guy is just too nice. Too reliable. Too . . . boring.

For some asinine reason, we women continually toss aside a nice guy in favor of someone who treats us like poo. We prefer to date a man who walks in front of us, doesn't introduce us to his friends, and only keeps beer in his fridge even though we've told him that we prefer wine. It seems that we women have something in common with the average weed: we thrive on neglect.

Sure, these nice guys may not have the same pizzazz as other men. They won't put us through the emotional highs and lows that we've grown so accustomed to enduring. Nice guys are courteous, not curt. They'll respect us, not reject us. And for a lot of us women, that just doesn't seem to cut it.

I do believe that nice guys are around for a reason. It's so that when we women wise up and get sick of being kicked in the heart over and over again by men that aren't worthy of us, we can go out and get ourselves a nice guy and set-tle down. And hopefully we can all live happily every after without all the drama and trauma. Sure, as the expression goes, nice guys finish last, but if you're ready to be with one of them, you may just find that your relationship with him may last as well.

Safety First!

The last point I want to make isn't as much a rule as it is common sense and it's something to keep in mind before ever going out. By far the scariest date that I've ever been on wasn't due to my escort's devil tattoo or facial scars, it was due to the fact that I thought that my life was in danger. Despite my better judgment, I let a first date pick me up even though I didn't know him very well. I didn't have any friends or family members that knew him either, so he came without any references. But he seemed nice enough at the time and because we were going to a concert and only had one parking pass, I decided to throw caution to the wind and let him drive.

The concert went okay. We had horrible seats and I could barely see who was performing even on the big screen, but all in all, it was fine. But then on the way home my date veered off the freeway onto a small, unfamiliar road that was definitely not on the way home. Panic set in. Where was he taking me? Was I going to survive? Would my last day on Earth really be the one I spent pretreating my wash and worse, skipped dessert? I felt helpless locked into the pas-senger seat not knowing if I should speak and if so, what to say that wouldn't set him into an angry rage. But then my panic ended when my would-be assassin realized that he had taken the wrong exit and got back on the freeway.

I learned a lesson that night that I will never forget. Always, and I mean always, take binoculars to any concert that you go to no matter how good the seats are. And of course, never let your date drive unless you're absolutely certain that he is of no danger to your well-being. If you do decide to go out with someone that you don't know very well, be smart and follow some age-old advice. Be sure to tell a friend where you'll be and what time you'll be home and bring enough money to get home safely. In addition, there are some new rules on the playing field that you should follow as well:

- Make sure that you Google your date before you go out with him. This way you'll know if your future soul mate has ever been an inmate.
- If you go somewhere for a drink, never take your eyes off of it. Unfortunately we live in a world where roofies are as available as Tylenol.
- At any point during the date, feel free to just say "No!" And say it as loudly and clearly as you possibly can.

And speaking of drinks, it's very common to mix alcohol with dating. If you do mix the two, keep in mind that you don't have the same memory skills when you've had one too many. Although beauty may be in the eye of the beholder, your eyes can't see straight if they're wearing beer goggles or rosé-colored glasses. The man you think is dreamy at 2:00 A.M. on a Friday can look like your worst nightmare when you meet him for dinner the following Tuesday. There are times I've woken up, remembered I had a great time the

night before, but couldn't quite visualize who made the evening so enjoyable. So when the guy calls me, I have a vague
idea who I'm talking to, but it's more like a police sketch
than an 8 × 10 glossy. So be smart and drink sensibly. Especially if you're going to be driving or making any kind of
decision. This ends my public service announcement.

Some Practical Advice

Things that you can do with all the dating books you bought
that promise you a husband if you simply follow their
advice:

1. Stack them on top of each other when you need help
   reaching the high shelf.
2. Find out the publishers and send them any manuscripts
   that you wrote. As you can tell, they'll publish just about
   anything.
3. Total up all the money that you wasted buying these
   books and purchase an equal amount of toilet paper. It
   will all wind up going down the drain as well.
4. Do the complete opposite of what they advise you to do.
   I'm sure that you'll have a much better chance of reaching your goal.
5. Give them as gifts to those women who men seem to
   flock to. Maybe now she'll scare them away and there'll
   be more men around for you.

chapter five

the first date: the hell you endure to get a free meal

First dates are like job interviews with beer nuts. They're painful and agonizing and bad for your health. The stress of them raises your blood pressure and puts more strain on your heart. Or at least it must. I've never actually read a study on it, but I guarantee you that if smoking one cigarette can take away seven minutes of your life, one first date can take away seven months.

But as bad as they may be for your health, it looks like you, my friend, are going to have one. Maybe it was the guy that you shared a latte with at Starbucks or the man that you shared a latke with at a Jewish mixer. Whoever he is, he's someone that's now in possession of your phone number and is going to call and ask you out. Although a small part of you is filled with excitement about the possibilities that this date could bring, the rest of you knows that this will just be a huge waste of time. Sure, this guy could turn out to be the one that you promise to love, honor, and cherish. But chances are better that he'll be the one to make you vow to never go on a date again and instead lead a celibate life raising sea monkeys.

But as depressing as a date may sound, at least you can be proud of yourself for taking a chance. You were proactive, gave out your phone number, and did something to change your eternity of available Saturday nights. Oprah would be so proud. But as exciting as the situation may be, and as much potential as it has, at some point it will hit you that you actually have to go out on a date! Instantly you're reminded of that famous expression, "Be careful what you wish for, for you just might get it" and you realize that truer words were never spoken.

But don't worry. It's very normal to feel this way. There's nothing wrong with you except your inability to take compliments and your habit of picking the slowest lane on the freeway. I don't know of even one person who enjoys going out on a first date. And why should they?

If you want even more proof that you're not alone in your hatred of first dates, take a look at your cell phone service. If you're a member of Cingular or Virgin Mobil, you can take advantage of their "Rescue Ring" or "Escape-a-Date" feature. With it, you program a time for your cell phone to ring during a date and you'll hear a computerized voice that will instruct you on what to say in order to flee the scene without any guilt. Cingular estimates that they place 10,000 of these preprogrammed calls per month. Not only does this tell me that plenty of other people despise first dates as well, but it saddens me to know that so many folks don't have a friend who can place such a call for free.

As you know, even if you actually like the guy that you're going out with, the first date will suck. Not only do you have the usual first-date stresses, but you also have the additional pressure of trying not to say anything stupid. This is a tough one for me since stupidity flows from me like hot lava from Mount Saint Helens. I remember in tenth grade biology, it was my turn to read aloud and I read the word "organism" as "orgasm" and everyone laughed at me. That's why to this day, if I go out with anyone cute, I refuse to say any word that begins with the letter *O*. I'm not so worried that he'll think that I'm an idiot; I'm more afraid that he'll see through my nervousness and realize that I like him. As you know, this would be the death of any budding relationship.

So what are these first-date stresses that you'll have to endure? Let's go through them one by one so that we can laugh and cry together in our own miserable state of despair. Let's go over some of the most uncomfortable, unnatural, and downright sucky things about going out with someone for the very first time.

He Pops the Question

Women may have all the power when it comes to deciding when to have sex for the first time, but it's the men who have the power when it comes to making that first phone call. And once you give your number to a guy, the wait begins. You try to keep yourself busy by thinking of more important things like last night's episode of *The O.C.*, but every time your phone rings, you stare at it like a deer in headlights. You try to be casual and let it ring a relaxed 2.5 times and then, in a rehearsed tone that's not too casual or not too excited, you say "hello?" Your heart stops for an instant while you wait for a response, but instead of hearing a seductive male voice, all you hear is a damned fax tone. Once again some unknown company is trying to send you junk mail via fax, but since you don't have a fax machine, they just keep calling and calling. You can't reach the company to tell them you don't have a fax machine since you don't know who they are or what their number is. So you spring for caller ID for the sole purpose of putting an end to this harassment, but all it says when they call is "Private Caller." I promise, I'll vote for any candidate that makes this his number one priority!

Then, just when you least expect it, your future date finally calls. Once you get past the initial awkwardness of him reminding you who he is and you pretending not to remember so he thinks guys call you all the time, the rest of your call goes surprisingly well. It's amazing how easy it can be to talk to someone you hardly know when you don't actually have to see his face. This fact of human nature is what porn lines that charge by the minute have relied on for years.

The only awkward part about this initial call is that you know that at some point during the conversation, he's going to ask you out. You wish he'd do it fast, like pulling off one of those home waxing strips. You don't want him to have enough time to chicken out or decide that, now that he's talked to you, he doesn't want to go out after all. Or worse, that you'll talk for so long that he'll get a call on his other line and will need to call you back! Then you're right back where you started, waiting for that damned phone to ring. In the end, he does ask you out and you accept his invitation. You did it! You're going on a date! Congratulations . . . I think.

Head, Shoulders, Knees, and Toes

You've heard the expression "It takes a village to raise a child," but did you also know that it takes a team of hairdressers, makeup artists, manicurists, pedicurists, and waxers to get you primed and ready to go out on a date? Depending on your look and your budget, you could literally spend a whole week, and a whole week's paycheck, getting yourself ready to go out on a date. Men don't realize how easy they have it when it comes to getting themselves all dolled up for the evening. They don't need to push back their cuticles. They don't need to minimize their pores. All they need to do to get ready for a date is to wipe off the drool from the corner of their mouths that they got from sleeping on the sofa all afternoon. For us, we often spend more time getting ready for the date than on the date itself. Let's take a full tour of what needs to get done, starting at our heads and working our way down.

First, we begin with our hair. Little do guys realize how much time, effort, and styling products it takes to give our hair that natural look. Having a good hair day isn't something that just happens. It entails flattening irons, styling gels, hair diffusers, curling irons, and a good volumizing mousse. It takes professional highlights, monthly root jobs, thinning shears, hair extensions, and deep-conditioning treatments. And of course, it also takes a favorable barometric reading of the humidity level to reduce potential frizz. Having a good hair day is like watching an Olympic athlete. In both cases, it takes a lot of time, effort, and practice to make it look so easy.

Moving south from our hair, we have the face to deal with. Makeup is another dating hurdle that needs to be reckoned with. I'm not one to wear much makeup in the first place. I always feel like a kid playing dress-up whenever I start painting my face. So whenever I put on my game face for a big date, I'd inevitably forget that I was wearing makeup and would rub my eyes until I looked like a battered wife. Maybe you have the opposite hurdle to deal with. I know many women who overdo their makeup before they go out. They wear so many layers of concealer, foundation, powder, rouge, and eye shadow that their necks actually hurt from holding up their heavy head.

Moving down to the neck, you need to decide if you want to wear perfume. It's been proven that the olfactory sense is the most powerful one of them all and that men are easily aroused by certain fragrances. Me, I'm easily confused by them. I can never decide which scent to choose. I've been sprayed and dabbed countless times at perfume counters and have inhaled so many odors that my bronchial tube smells like a floral bouquet. If I ever do find a scent that I like, do I get the perfume, the eau de cologne, the lotion, or the toilet water? It's all much too confusing. I have a hard enough time deciding between paper or plastic. If you want my opinion, I'd forget perfume altogether. If you really want a scent that a man can't resist, dab a little BBQ sauce behind each ear.

The skin on your body is another complex issue. You want it to be as soft as a baby's hiney, so you shave it, exfoliate it, and apply so much moisture to it that it's dewy enough to sustain sea life. And speaking of moisturizers, they've been perfected to a whole new level. They've added sunscreen to prevent skin damage, glycolic agents to prevent wrinkles, and some kind of product that I don't even want to know about that allows you to shave less often. So make sure that you lather on plenty of moisturizer. You don't want to scare away any guy because of sunburn, wrinkles, or flaky skin around your kneecap area.

As we spread out from the body to our appendages, we have to do something to spruce up our nails. For some, this may simply mean applying a clear coat of polish, but for others it's a trip to the salon for acrylic fills, manicures, pedicures, and French tips. Some women like to turn each nail into its own little Sistine Chapel by having the manicurist paint on flowers, astrological symbols, or cute little animals. Then they apply rhinestones and other festive touches that make their nails light up like little Christmas trees.

Then there's the whole vaginal area to think about. Do you let the hair on it grow wild like a forest or do you wax it off like a mountain that's been devastated by a forest fire? Some women prefer that it be clipped into little Disneyland topiaries. And still others have this strange behavior that I'll never understand of douching before a hot date and deodorizing themselves until they're clean enough to eat off of . . . oh wait, now I get it.

And just when we think we're safe to go out into the dating world, there are some last-minute touches that only a good pair of tweezers can provide. Your eyebrows will need to be plucked, the hairs on your big toe will need to be eliminated, and that stray hair that grows from your chin like a giant redwood will need to be chopped down. As you can see, there is an endless list of body parts that need tending to before you date, and, just like painting the Golden Gate Bridge, by the time you're finished doing it, it's time to start the whole process all over again

Dress to Obsess

Finding the perfect outfit to wear on a first date is like trying to find a cure for the common cold. Medical researchers have battled this one for years but still people walk around with a noseful of snot come winter. The reason that finding the perfect outfit is a mystery as well is that there are too many uncertainties. First of all, even though you know that you're going out to dinner, you don't know what restaurant you'll be going to. As you know, you need an entirely different ensemble for a French bistro than you do to grab a couple of chimichangas. Another problem is that you want your date to think you look nice, but you don't know what type of look he's into. Does he prefer one that you'd find on a runway, or one that you'd find on a runaway working the streets? And finally, you have no idea what your date's going to wear; you don't want to show up in a suit when he's dressed in a mesh tank top and cutoffs.

You peruse your closet in search of that perfect outfit that makes you look ten pounds lighter and two cup sizes larger. You sift through hanger after hanger looking for something that isn't too old, tight, trendy, or retro. If you can't find anything in your closet, you see if you can borrow something from a friend, or better yet, hit the mall!

Wearing something new on a date gives you that extra boost of confidence that you can only get from buying retail. But that boost is short-lived and only works the first time you wear it. Once that new article of clothing has been washed, its power fades as fast as new-car smell.

> “Whenever I'm trying to decide what to wear, I'm always tempted to wear my old worn-out jeans. It'd be like bringing my comfy baby blankie with me.”
>
> —Alexis

But you should be warned about a fashion injustice that takes place at the mall. It seems that department stores commonly use mirrors that are similar to those used in carnival fun houses. But instead of transforming your body into a freakishly contorted form, it distorts it into that of Naomi Watts. Suddenly you're tall and thin and have a strong desire to chain-smoke. You can't believe how amazing you look in your outfit and even buy it in three different colors. But once you put it on for your big date, you stare at your reflection in horror as if you're Cinderella and it's one minute after midnight.

As if selecting an outfit isn't hard enough, you also have to decide on the right undergarments. Do you need a thong to hide any panty lines or boy-cut briefs to avoid indecent exposure charges while standing on a balcony in a miniskirt? Do you need a padded bra to give your cleavage a boost or one made out of a thicker material to hide your nipples in even the coldest Arctic climate? Or maybe you need a body-slimming girdle that locks your fat in place like a house bolted to its foundation. I've come to realize that Victoria's real secret is that she's raking in the dough while creating a crapload of products for us to agonize about.

Once you find a good first-date outfit, you may want to do what my friend Cindy did. Cindy wore that same outfit on every one of her first dates. She found a perfect outfit that worked well in both casual and more formal settings. It was the right balance of being seductive without being slutty. It was made from a stretchy material so it fit no matter what time of the month it was. And it was black, so it helped hide the damage caused by her passion for Krispy Kremes.

Cindy applied her strict dating attire to future dates as well. She had preselected good outfits for second and third dates and would wear them in strict procession, as though she were a Karate student working her way up the chain of colored belts. This way she would never wear the same outfit twice with any of her dates. Unfortunately, Cindy rarely got to wear her third-date outfit. She said it was because the guys were scared off by her intelligence, but between you and me, I think it had more to due with her anal-retentive nature.

Your Dating To-Do List

Going on a date is no simple task. It involves numerous chores, errands, and prep work. In a way, getting ready for a date is not unlike what a chef goes through to prepare a ten-course gourmet feast. In both instances, there are an overwhelming amount of things to do. Sure, we just discussed two of the biggies, but in order to achieve the many other things, I've put together a list.

Some of the things on the list can be done days ahead of time, and others need to be done at the very last minute. Because of the hectic dating-prep schedule, you need to be extremely organized and this list can help that goal. Here is a basic dating schedule that you can use as a guideline in order for your big night out to go off without a hitch.

Immediately after you hang up the phone, you should:

1. Call your best friend and tell her everything that he said and everything that you said and what he said after you said what it was that you said.
2. If you have kids, start calling in favors and begging friends and family in hopes of finding a sitter for that impossible Saturday night.

3. Go on the Internet and Google your date. This is a great way to find out if he has a criminal record or owes any outstanding child support payments. You can also tell if he really is a doctor like he told you, or if he just meant that he likes to play doctor.
4. Start agonizing over what to wear.
5. Regret ever saying yes.

A few days before the date, you:

1. Finalize your outfit. If you can't find a good one in your closet, hit the malls or borrow something from a friend.
2. Go to the gym and work out like a fiend to rid yourself of a years' worth of overindulgence in only a few short days.
3. Get a manicure and pedicure to help give the illusion that you care about your appearance, when in fact you've been wearing the same pair of socks for three days because you're too lazy to go to the store to buy more detergent.
4. Bleach or wax any facial hair that needs bleaching or waxing.
5. Renew your prescription for Prozac.
6. Dread the date even more.

The day of the date, be sure to:

1. Kick yourself in the head for ever agreeing to go out on this stupid thing in the first place.
2. Wash your hair over and over again until it comes out just right. While you're in the shower shave your pits and legs and any place else in between that you feel needs shaving.

3. If he's going to pick you up, straighten up your apartment. Hide any issues of Bride's magazine that you may have lying around.

4. Put away ugly pictures of yourself. Cut out photos of male models and put them in frames so that your date thinks these guys are your exes.

5. Go through your medicine cabinet and bathroom cupboards and hide any yeast cream, hemorrhoid pads, and feminine hygiene products. Check the bathroom for any wayward pubic hairs.

An hour before the date, you will:

1. Feel nauseous.

2. Put on your makeup. Don't forget to cover up that huge zit that appeared this morning because you've been stressed out about the date all week.

3. Pluck that thick stray hair that grows on your chin.

4. If you think that there's a chance for sex, change your sheets, put protection in your purse, and check your bikini line. Remember to put on a sexy bra and underwear.

5. If you think there's a chance for sex and you don't want to be tempted, toss the condoms and wear really ugly granny pants.

6. Get dressed.

A few minutes before the date, you will no doubt:

1. Find a run in your hose. Desperately search for another pair only to discover that you don't have any that match your outfit. Decide to rethink the outfit and go with socks and boots. Change your skirt because it's too "go-

go" like with the boots. The new longer skirt clashes with the blouse, so a quick change into a turtleneck. Head toward bathroom to repair messed up hair caused by putting on the turtleneck. Notice in mirror that your mascara was smudged when you put on the turtleneck. Damn that turtleneck. Remove smudge with wet Q-tip. There. Now you look presentable but your place is a disaster. Clean up again.

2. Swear to God that you will never, and you mean never, go out on a date again.

Take a Second to Make a First Impression

Now that the agony of deciding what to wear is behind you, you have another stress point to deal with. You need to figure out what to do when your date arrives. Sure, you can just do whatever normal activity you'd be doing on a Saturday night, but I don't think he'd be all that impressed watching you study your face in a magnifying mirror while you watch a plastic surgery documentary.

What you need to do is create an environment that gives your date the appearance of you leading a full and satisfying life without a man while still remaining feminine and vulnerable. It's a delicate balancing act and you have to be as adept at it as Carly Patterson. You have to decide what message that you want to convey about yourself and the best way of conveying it.

What You Can Be Doing When He Arrives

Activity	What the Activity Says about You
Talking on the phone	You have a lot of friends in your life to keep you busy so you're not desperate to find a guy. If you can manage to give a hearty laugh while on the phone, all the better.
Listening to music	You're cool and have plenty of deep thoughts to entertain yourself without watching TV. Of course, you still have to decide if you want to listen to jazz or rap or anything in between, so that can be a whole other ball of wax.
Watching a sporting event	You have a tomboy side to your personality, and you have an interest in common with your date. I bet you'd be equally intrigued if you went to his house and he was watching Soap Network.
Doing the crossword	You're smart. Of course, this only works if you have actual answers filled in the puzzle.
Reading a book	You're well read and educated, assuming that the book you're reading doesn't have a picture of Fabio on the cover.
Frantically putting on your shoes	This conveys that this date is no big deal and that you just threw your outfit together at the last minute.
Baking	You're the domestic type who enjoys doing things around the house. In addition, the aroma works as a wonderful aphrodisiac.

Ding-Dong, Your Date Is Here!

No matter what activity you choose to partake in, don't be surprised if you can't concentrate on it very well. You know that at any second your doorbell will ring and it will shock your heart like a set of defibrillating paddles. You try to let your mind wander but all you can think about is that for the first time ever, you can actually feel your hair turning gray.

And then it happens. The doorbell rings. The moment that you've been waiting for has finally arrived. If you're lucky, you have one of those little peephole thingies built into your front door so that you can take a look at your date. If you don't, all you can do is hope for the best. You know that it will take but a millisecond after you open that door to know if you're going to enjoy the next several hours, of if you'd rather stay home and gnaw off your tongue. I'm not saying that your date has to be a gorgeous hunk of burning love in order for you to have a good time, but it sure doesn't hurt.

You take a breath, head toward the door, and ponder whether you should greet this guy with a handshake, a hug, or a peck on the cheek. You open the door, put on your best fake smile, and decide that the peck would work best. But as you lean into him, he's surprised by this movement, and turns his head so that you end up kissing his eyelid. Here you are, not even three seconds into the date and already you're smack dab in awkward hell. Get used to it. The date has only just begun.

Driving in Cars with a Boy

At some point after your date arrives, it will be time to leave your place. Maybe it'll be after the two of you have a drink. Or maybe you'll decide to skip the drink altogether and opt to get the hell out of there so that you'll be home that much faster. But at some point, the two of you will be out the door and on your way to your destination.

Your date offers to drive, so you stroll down the street toward his car. Since you have no idea what kind of car he drives, you walk past each vehicle in silence, waiting for him to stop and get out his keys. You walk by a brand-new black BMW. Nothing. A sporty two-seater convertible. Nada. You feel like you're on a game show waiting for Johnny to tell you what you've won. Finally, you claim your prize as your date stops in front of a beat-up jalopy that's held together by duct tape.

Your date opens the door for you . . . or maybe he doesn't . . . and you climb inside. From this moment on, you're in foreign territory. You're like a Doberman pinscher sniffing out clues that will give you an insight into your date's true personality. Hmmm, you don't see any weapons or possible gags, so you relax a bit into your sticky bucket seat. But just because there isn't any ammo lying about doesn't mean that there aren't any danger signs. Here are some of those red flags to look out for:

- Are there trash and fast-food wrappers lying about or did he take the time to clean out his car before he picked you up? Believe me, if he didn't clean out his car, you can forget about him ever cleaning up after himself. Do you really want to spend the rest of your life picking up after a grown man?

- Does he have a radar detector clipped to his overhead mirror? If so, he's probably had some tickets in his past or maybe even has some warrants out for his arrest. He may be a fast-driving, reckless kind of man who doesn't care much about his own safety or the safety of others. Does this sound like a good father for your future children?

❝ I once got into my date's car and noticed that there was a bottle of iced tea lying by my feet. When I picked it up to toss it in the back, I realized that it wasn't a bottle of iced tea after all. It was more like a spittoon with the remnants of his last dip of Skoal. **❞**

—Meridith

- Is his ashtray full of cigarette butts? If so, he's obviously a smoker, which is fine if you are, but if not, do you really want to fall in love with someone who smells like rot?
- Does he have one of those pen and pad thingies stuck to his dashboard and a hands-free cell phone holder? If so, he may be a workaholic and uses his car as a mobile office. Not only does this make for more fender benders, it may limit his interest in any conversation that doesn't include the Dow Jones average.

Although I've had my share of memorable car rides with boys, I'd have to say the most memorable one was with this man who had a passion for racing. For some strange reason he gave me the nickname of "Tiger" as soon as I stepped foot in his car. I didn't quite understand why, unless that's the translation of my name in NASCAR-speak. But even worse than my nickname was the car ride itself. As soon as my date was in his car, his body developed a nervous tic. His right shoulder would spasm whenever he put the car into gear and I was terrified that he'd throw the car into reverse at any moment. From that day on I decided only to date men who drove automatics.

Date-Place Disasters

When a guy asks you out for the first time, you can pretty much count on him taking you to a restaurant or a bar or anywhere else where hard liquor is served. But once in a while, you'll find a guy who deviates from this traditional path and chooses a more creative venue. By doing so, he hopes to impress you into thinking that there's more to him than your average Joe. Even though this technique shows that he can think outside the box, some of the places that he can take you will make you wish that he actually took you to a box so that you could climb inside of it until the date ends.

Whenever I've gone out with a guy and he suggested one of these "off the beaten path" kind of places, I just wimpishly said, "Sure, that sounds fun." But what I was really thinking was, "Oh man, this is going to suck big time!" If you're like me and don't speak your mind unless something major happens like getting carob chips on your yogurt when you distinctly asked for cookie crumbs, following are some of the suckier places that you can expect to go on your date.

A Bowling Alley

Unless you're a good bowler, spending your first date at a bowling alley is always a bad idea. Sure your date will like it because he can check out your ass when it's your turn to bowl, but everything about the place is uncomplimentary to you. The lighting is harsh. The shoes are ugly. And you look like a dumb girl making all those gutter balls. I'm sure that your date will offer to teach you how to throw the ball correctly so that you can knock down more pins, but all he really wants to do is to nuzzle up behind you so you can feel his own pin.

A Party

I'd avoid going to a party on the first date unless it's a party that's given by your friends. If you go to a party with his friends, there are too many uncertainties. Will it be in a safe part of town? Will there be any illegal drugs? Will there be good hors d'oeuvres? Also, if it's a party that only he knows about, chances are you won't know any of the guests. Hell, you'll barely even know your own date. Does that sound like a good time had by all? I don't think so.

A Movie

I'm a big fan of movies. I love the stories. I love the stars. And most of all I love the bulk candy. But the only time that I don't think it's a great idea to go to a movie is when you're on a first date. The main problem with going to a movie is that there's hardly any time for you to talk to your date. Sure, you can chat beforehand when they play that trivia game on the screen, but I actually kind of like that part. It makes up for the stupidity I feel watching *Jeopardy* and not being able to answer the questions. Also, if the movie is a violent one, the blood and gore could turn you off. And worse, if it's a sexy movie, the frontal nudity will turn him on!

A Batting Cage

There are two reasons that a man would take a woman to a batting cage. The first one is obvious: men like to see women in a cage. They prefer them to wear go-go boots, but they're not strict on that point. The other is that it gives them the upper hand. Since men have been playing baseball since they were boys, they know how to swing a bat with grace and style and hope to woo us with this macho quality. Unfortunately, all we feel is self-conscious because the batting helmet gives us such terrible hat hair.

A Sporting Event

Unless you like the specific sporting event, I'd give this one a pass too. I once went to a hockey game on a first date and had the worst time of my life. Not only did I find the sport to be incredibly boring, I found my date to be incredibly gross. He had a habit of kissing me whenever his team scored a goal. Normally this wouldn't be much of a problem since the average hockey game has the score of one to nothing. But this must have been the highest-scoring hockey game in history. It was like 93 to 105.

A Hike

Although this may sound romantic, it's anything but. To begin with, the attire isn't the most flattering and if you wear makeup it'll just melt down your face like wax on a hot day. The trails can be hot and dusty, and you run the risk of being bitten by bugs and snakes or stepping on poison ivy. In the end, you're just plain sweaty, itchy, and bitchy, and there's nothing very sexy about that. So if a guy wants to hit the trails on your first date, tell him to go take a hike.

A Nightclub

Maybe it's just me, but a nightclub is the last place that I'd want to go on a first date. I'm not the best dancer in the world, so unless I'm stinking drunk, I don't like to dance. It's not that the alcohol makes me dance any better, it just makes me care a lot less. Also, clubs are so loud that you can't hear each other talk—which, now that I think about it, may not be such a bad thing if you don't like the guy that you're with.

This is only a partial list of extracurricular first-date activities that your date can suggest. God knows there are plenty others. One guy brought me to a wax museum. Another took me with him to test-drive cars. And there was the guy who brought me to the park to ride the kiddie trains. All I can say is that if a man suggests going to a place that's off the beaten path for your first date, he deserves a beatin' himself.

Let's Give Him Something to Talk About

Men may have women beat when it comes to upper-body strength and knowing how to hook up an audio system, but when it comes to being able to carry on a conversation, we have them licked hands down. The reason is caused by the difference in our wiring. Men are taught to keep their emotions inside. They avoid confrontation at all cost and believe that there are things that are best left unsaid. Women, on the other hand, never run out of things to say and can talk any subject to death. That is, of course, if they're talking to another woman.

But if we're trying to converse with a guy on a date, then all bets are off. We sit across from him telling him about our lives and our goals and our dreams of owning a cottage by the sea, but he just sits there like a Marcel Marceau. The only thing he offers up is a stream of awkward pauses and

occasional grunts. Trying to get a man to talk on a first date
is as futile as trying to get him to lactate.

But there is a little secret that I want to let you in on that
will enable you to alter your date's internal wiring. There
is one topic of conversation that will make him ramble on
and on like a first-time Oscar winner. Do you want to know
what it is? Do you? Huh? Do you? Well . . . drumroll please.
. . . If you want your date to start talking, ask him anything
at all to do with himself! It's really just that simple. Once
you ask him about his job or his home or his family, he'll get
infected with a good case of diarrhea of the mouth.

Unfortunately, after you get him going, you're the one
that's going to end up getting sick, because your date will
talk on and on ad nauseam. You won't be able to get him
to stop. He's like a weak Atkins dieter in front of a bag of
Cheetos. And don't for one minute think that if he goes
on and on about his life that he'll give you the courtesy
of letting you talk about yours. I'm not quite sure why a
man's own life holds such vast interest for him. I guess I'll
have to chalk it up to the other things in life that I'll never
understand, like how a multiton airplane can float on a
cushion of air.

But be warned that your date's total obsession with
himself is a condition that's very short-lived. This diarrhea
of the mouth cures itself after your very first date. In fact, if
you two ever end up getting together, his mouth will once
again become constipated. From here on in, you can expect
a lifetime of trying to get him to say something, anything,
ever again. He'll remain forever zoned-out in front of the
tube while you yell and scream and nag at him in hopes of
getting any kind of a response. I wish that I had a magic

topic of conversation to offer at that point, because if I did, I'd make a fortune and could buy myself my own cottage by the sea.

Food Frustrations

I always found that one of the most unappealing aspects of going out to dinner on a first date was the dinner itself. I'd get so nervous that the thought of food would disgust me as much as Liza Minnelli's wedding kiss with David Gest. At all other times I have a wonderful, hearty appetite and can eat just about anything that's placed in front of me—except banana chips. I once ate an entire bag of them at one sitting and now I find them as disgusting as, well, Liza Minnelli's wedding kiss with David Gest.

As we have already discussed, dating is a nerve-racking experience, and I find it difficult to eat when my nerves are racking. This is yet another example of the many differences between the sexes. Men have a veracious appetite and can eat no matter what the circumstances. Just look at a prisoner on death row ordering his last meal. There he is, an hour away from being given a lethal injection of poison, and he's chowin' down his grub like he's at a tailgate party.

On a date, food isn't just food anymore. There's so much more importance placed upon it that deciding what to order can give you brain freeze. For instance, because you aren't that hungry, all you may want is a small appetizer. But if that's what you order, your date will think that you have an eating disorder (of course, he'll also be thrilled that you're such a cheap date). If you opt for a full meal and don't finish it, he'll think you're the kind of woman who doesn't mind wasting money. And if you order something expensive, he'll assume you'll be one of those wives who does nothing but sit around all day waiting for their QVC packages to arrive.

To make matters even more confusing, you don't want to order any kind of food that will embarrass you. You shy away from spinach because it could stick in your teeth. You don't want anything that splatters, like spaghetti sauce, or else you'll end up wearing it. And above all, you have to deny yourself any food that causes gas or you'll wind up looking like the girl who swelled up like a giant blueberry after chewing bubble gum in *Willy Wonka and the Chocolate Factory*.

If that's not enough to make you wish you'd only ordered water, there's another problem that may arise. What if the food that you're served isn't the food that you ordered? Maybe it tastes horrible or they put something in it that you asked them to hold. Now you're faced with the decision of whether to eat it or to send it back. If you eat it, you make yourself sick; if you send it back, you open up yet another can of worms. Does your date eat his meal or wait for your new meal to arrive? If he waits, his meal will get cold; if he eats, he'll be done with his food by the time yours arrives. Not only is this an awkward situation, but it also prolongs the date.

As you can see, there's enough stress caused by eating dinner on your first date to give you an ulcer. And heaven forbid that happens, because the next time you go on a first date, you'll be even more restricted when ordering your meal. This, of course, will add even more stress, which will cause even more ulcers—and the pattern will continue until you're married or turn into one big open sore.

Check Please

At some point after your plates are taken away, the waiter will come by and place the check in the middle of your table. This, my friend, is one of the most universally uncomfortable moments of any date. The reason this is so awkward is that even if your date asked you out, you can't always assume that he'll pay. So you both just sit there trying to ignore the bill as if it were Donald Trump's combover.

One factor in determining who doles out the dough is where the date takes place. If you go on a date anywhere else but New York and Los Angeles, you can expect to get your Bloomin' Onion for free. Generally, men who have been raised in between those two cities have been brought up by strong mothers with good old-fashioned values. In fact, if you offer to pay for a date, these men will probably refuse. So sit back, relax, and enjoy the hospitality, as well as that yummy onion thing!

On the other hand, if you go out with a man in either New York or Los Angeles, the choice of who pays is one big crapshoot. In both of these modern cities there are far less manners, far less dating rules, and, of course, far less parking places close to the restaurant.

Another factor to take into account is who ate what. I hate it when my date orders a shrimp cocktail, a porterhouse steak, and cherries jubilee, and all I have is a garden salad, and he wants to split the check. I know that if the meals were reversed, I would offer to pay the check. Sure, you may not agree with me, but your stomach may not agree with *you* after you ate such a heavy meal before bedtime.

Personally, I have my own deciding factor that determines who should pay that overrides all of the other ones.

That factor is how much I like my date. If I know that I have no interest in ever going out with the guy again, I always offer to chip in or even pay for the entire dinner. That way I feel no obligation toward this guy and even feel less guilty saying no if he asks me out again. I also feel that he has less of a chance of becoming an angry stalker if I pay for his cashew chicken.

But many women disagree with my logic. They feel that they've already invested a lot of money into the evening. They bought a new hair product, used some of their expensive perfume, and even had to dry-clean their outfit at the end of the evening. No matter if they like the guy or not, they're going to get a free meal out of it to even things out.

Now What?

The food has been eaten. The small talk's exhausted. The check has been paid. You think that you're home free until he utters those painful words, "So, what do you want to do now?" What you really want to do is "date and dash" and crawl under your comfy sheets made out of T-shirt material, but before you can make up an excuse, he pushes the issue even more. "I know a coffeehouse down the street that has the best lemon tart in the city. Let's go!" Wasting time is one thing, but wasting calories is another. Feign exhaustion, and end it, before you sink deeper into dating hell.

I propose that there be dating signals not unlike those that a catcher gives to a pitcher to tell him what kind of pitch to throw. A catcher has a signal for a fastball, one for a curve ball, and one that looks like a signal but actually just means that he has an itch on his privates. If there were signals for dating, it would make the process far less uncomfortable for all concerned. Some examples would be:

Signals for Dating

Signal	What It Means
Tap your watch	I have to go home to feed my cat, water my plants, or plan for my tax audit. Anything that's more exciting than spending more time with you.
Touch your forehead	I have a headache from being bored silly for the past five hours and need more mental stimulation like watching paint dry to make me feel better.
Put your hands to your neck and pretend to choke yourself	Just kill me now. I can't bear to date anymore and want to end it all right this instant.

One note of caution: If your date invites you up for a cup of coffee, realize that the last thing he wants to do is actually have a cup of coffee. And the same holds true for you. If you invite him up for a drink, realize that your date will read a lot more into the invite. People hear what they want to hear and when you say, "Do you want a Budweiser?" all he'll hear is "Do you want a blowjob?"

The Goodnight Kiss

As if all the trauma of a first date weren't enough, then you have to deal with the goodnight kiss, which can be particularly dreadful if you're out with a guy who you have no interest in kissing. The worst kind is when your date drives you home and parks in front of your house. He kills the engine and makes no attempt to get out of the car. At this point, you know you're screwed. Your date just sits there trying to gather up his courage to make his move. You squirm like a mouse in a python's cage desperately searching for an escape route. Then suddenly he licks his lips, looks down at yours for aim, and goes in for the kill. Ugh! Don't you just hate when that happens?

But even if you like the guy that you're out with, the goodnight kiss can still be an incredibly stressful event. You have to convey your interest in him without saying a word, all the while trying to decipher if he has any interest in you. If you see him leaning toward you, you have but an instant to determine if he's going to kiss you or he's about to tie his shoe. If you get it wrong, you'll be mortified and your date will stumble out of there and possibly out of your life forever.

If you don't like the guy, the goodnight kiss can be even worse, but for an entirely different reason: it can make you physically sick. Kissing is a very personal matter, and you don't want to do it with every Tom, Dick, and hairy man that you meet. Even worse, giving a kiss to a bad date is misleading and he could easily read into it that you like him. Then he'll inevitably ask you that dreaded question of, "So, can I see you again?" This question is like the one about which came first, the chicken or the egg. There simply is no right answer. If you tell him no, you feel horrible for hurting his feelings. And if you say yes, then you've convinced him that you're interested even when you're not.

As you can see, that goodnight kiss can be one of the most awkward and uncomfortable parts of going out on a first date. But the one joy that it does bring, no matter how bad the kiss was or how far he shoved his tongue down your throat, is that it signifies the end of the evening. The date is over and you have survived. Sure, you've lessened your life-span by those seven months, but for now you're happy.

Best Free Meals

Make the most of the free meal if you can. Here are my suggestions of what to order to make the most out of it:

1. Any kind of risotto: It's so creamy and delicious and such a pain in the ass to make at home.
2. Fish: Whenever you make fish at home, it takes about a week for the stink to go away.
3. Vegetable soup: Same reason as fish.
4. A panini sandwich: Who can rationalize the expense of $1,000 for a panini maker?
5. An espresso-based coffee drink like a cappuccino or latte: Sure, you could buy espresso coffee and an espresso maker, but I find that they never taste as good and the foam is never as creamy when you make them at home.

chapter six

post-traumatic date disorder

Hip, hip hooray! The date from hell is finally over and you're back in your warm cozy home once again! You can't imagine that Nelson Mandela felt any better coming home after all those years of wrongful incarceration. Assuming that you had a bad date (which is usually a pretty good assumption), you've wasted several hours of your life as well as many layers of good makeup.

But what if the guy that you went out with wasn't a total loser? If this is true, then your dating saga has only just begun. Now you need to move on to the next step, which is deciding if this guy is worthy of going out with a second time. You know what needs to be done. It's the only thing that a single girl in your position can possibly do when faced with such a challenge: call your best friend and judge this guy on every possible level.

The two of you need to examine every aspect of your date as if it were the murder scene on an episode of *CSI*. You must go over his outfit looking for trace evidence of geekiness. You need to recount every syllable of your conversation looking for every possible red flag. You can't give up until the end credits roll.

I know that some people would accuse you of being too picky. They think you're overly harsh when judging if a guy is worthy of a second date, but I disagree with them. In fact, I don't think there is such a thing as being too judgmental when it comes to deciding if a guy's worth spending time with. Sure, others may not agree and they're welcome to their opinions no matter how wrong they are, but I'll stand firm on this one. In fact, I've always been astounded by such people. Why shouldn't a girl be picky when choosing someone to be close to? If things work out, you're going to share your body and soul with this man for the rest of your life, not to mention half of your bathroom mirror space each morning as you get dressed for work.

Granted, not all women are as picky when it comes to men. Some spend more time choosing a melon then they do a dinner date. But there is nothing wrong with being picky, as long as you realize that you're never going to find a guy who's 100 percent perfect. Unfortunately, there is no man out there who will satisfy every trait on your list of what you want in a man. If you ever do find a George Clooney for yourself, chances are that there'll be a little George Costanza mixed in.

❝I went out to dinner with this guy once who had so much chest hair that it started to pop through his shirt halfway through dinner.❞

—Mary

Pick Your No's

I know that I've rejected a lot of guys either because they didn't live up to my standards or they bugged the hell out of me. And, even though it goes against the advise from dear old mom, dad, grandma, and every book in the self-help aisle, I don't ever think you should go out with a guy if you feel like there's something wrong with him. And, oh, how many things there can be. Take a look.

Physical Turnoffs

Women are a lot more forgiving then men are when it comes to accepting certain unattractive physical characteristics. We know that we have to put up with a few flaws simply because there aren't enough good-looking men to go around. Also, from an evolutionary standpoint, women are supposed to be more attracted to a man that can give her children a stable home rather than one that can give her kids wavy hair and cleft chins. But that doesn't mean that even we don't have our limits. Here are some that warrant tossing him away:

He has excess chest hair: The amount of acceptable chest hair a man can have is a very personal preference. Some women like their man's chest to look like Chewbacca's from *Star Wars*, while others prefer it to be more like one of those hairless cats. Me, I favor less hair. The way I see it, if a guy's chest is full of hair, it has the tendency to spread to the rest of him like a skin-eating bacteria.

He just plain smells bad: Once in a while you'll come across a guy who emits a very unpleasant stench. It's not a manly musky smell but more of a rancid rotting odor that oozes from every pore in his skin. He's like King Midas, but instead of making everything he touches turn to gold, he makes everything he touches smell like mold.

He has bad feet: Oh, there are so many things that can go wrong with a guy's feet. To begin with, they can reek so bad that they smell like . . . well, feet. Also, many guys neglect to cut their toenails, so they grow long and thick like rhinoceros horns. These nails can be riddled with fungus and can crack and turn green. Isn't that attractive? I think not!

He has tattoos: I'm fine with a tasteful tattoo or two (try saying that three times fast), but when a guy has turned his body into the Norton Simon Museum, I draw the line.

He has a dead, missing, or gold front tooth: A great smile is not only sexy, it's also a good indication of how well a guy takes care of himself. If your date is reluctant to show off his pearly whites, it may be a sign that his whites have faded to gray. If he doesn't take care of himself and brush, floss, and visit the dentist regularly, don't expect him to take much care of you.

He makes a noise when he chews: I'm very sensitive to certain sounds, and it bothers me when a guy's jaw cracks whenever he eats his food. Who wants to be forced to wear earplugs at the dinner table to drown out the sound of your date's chewing?

He has a pasty white buildup in the corner of his mouth: Do I really have to clarify this one any further?

He sweats profusely: I accept the fact that a man's body temperature runs a bit warmer than a woman's, but what

I can't accept is a guy who sweats so much that he leaves a trail behind him like a snail. If you're with a guy who's constantly overheated, you can expect to do a mountain of laundry, have constant battles over the thermostat setting, and have a guy that's just plain icky to touch.

He's a loud breather: This goes back to my sensitivity to sounds. I couldn't imagine spending the rest of my life with someone who bugs me every time he takes a breath. I can't even stay through a movie if I'm sitting next to someone like this.

He has bad breath: When I say bad breath, I'm not talking about the mild kind that's brought on by eating too much garlic and spicy food. I'm talking about the constant and foul stink that inhabits a guy's mouth as if something has crawled underneath his tongue and died.

He resembles my father: I know Freud said that women marry men who remind them of their fathers, and while this may be true, I don't know of any who marry men that actually look like their father. I went out on a blind date once with a guy that looked very much like my dad. Throughout the evening the only urge I fought was the one to ask him if I could borrow some money.

Bad Manners

I'm not much of a stickler for etiquette. I've been known to put my elbows on the table and not send out thank-you cards in a quick and timely manner. But there are certain behaviors that I simply couldn't tolerate in a potential spouse. When it comes to guys, I'm a realist. I know that men have limits when it comes to being mature. I know they think comedy about bodily functions is the highest form of humor, and I don't expect any one of them to lay his jacket over a puddle for me to step onto. But there are some common courtesies that I do expect. And others, like the following, that I could easily do without:

He farts without hesitation: I went out with a guy once who kept farting at the dinner table. I was completely dumb-founded by this. I don't know if he had a physical problem or if he just thought that I didn't hear him. Either way I was very sickened by it, probably due to the fact that I held my breath for so long that I killed millions of my own brain cells. I'm sure that Emily Post didn't blame me one bit for tossing that guy into the waste heap.

He hawks up loogies: I never understood a man's casual atti-tude toward drawing mucus down from his sinus cavity and spitting it out. To these men, this disgusting behavior is as acceptable as scratching an itch. But to me, it's a definite reason to scratch him off my list of men.

He has hands like an octopus: I'm okay with guys who have two left feet, but I'm repulsed by the ones who have eight right hands. These flailing hands invade you without per-mission, not unlike Bush did with the Iraqi war.

He flirts with the waitress: It can never be a good sign when your date pays more attention to the waitress than he does to you. If you confront him, he'll only tell you that he does it to get better service. And if you fall for his answer, you're doing yourself a huge disservice.

❝I went out with this guy once who seemed to be okay, but I just couldn't get past this one thing. He had a horrible name. Dick. I just couldn't imagine introducing him to my friends and family without laughing and I could never say his name in the throws of passion.**❞**

—Amy

He burps loudly: I know that in some countries a loud burp at the end of the meal is seen as a compliment. But in this country, the only thing it's seen as is rude. I can forgive him if he follows it up by an apology, but when it's followed by another burp in the tune of the National Anthem, I say bye-bye to this belching boy.

He talks with his mouth full: I'm all for knowing what's really inside a man, but not when it comes to what's inside his mouth. Seeing a guy's food bolus is more intimacy than even I can take.

He picks his teeth with weird things: I've seen it all when it comes to this department. I've seen a guy use a matchstick to get in between there, a fork tong, the edge of the table-cloth, and even a strand of his own hair. I've seen a guy use everything: everything, that is, except for a toothpick.

He does drugs: If you do drugs yourself and/or aren't both-ered by a guy that does, fine by me. But I was raised by parents who openly did drugs when I was a kid and my way of rebelling was to become a big ol' square. I only drink on occasion and my drug of choice is Nyquil because it's "the stuffy head, fever, so I can sleep medicine."

He whistles incessantly: I know it's just my sensitivity to sounds acting up again, but when a guy whistles through his teeth, to me it sounds like nails on a chalkboard. I'm not really one to talk since I'm a constant hummer, but when it comes to dating, I should be allowed to do anything that I want to do while regulating each and every one of his behaviors.

Personality Traits

Because women tend to be more forgiving than men in the looks department, we're probably less forgiving when it comes to accepting a guy's bad personality. We figure that if we have to put up with someone who's short and plump and has more moles than an eighteen-hole golf course, we shouldn't have to put up with rude personality traits like these as well.

An artsy-fartsy type: He's fun to date in college. You smoke together and drink cheap wine. But in the end, personally I need more in a man than a tofu lovin', antiestablishment kind of guy who never has money, isn't fond of personal grooming, and prefers to leave the bathroom door open.

An "ic" man: I don't care if he's an alcoholic, a drug addict, a sex-aholic, or a workaholic, a man with an addictive personality isn't the kind of guy that I'm going to crave. I've done it before; I went out with a guy who was trying to quit doing drugs. I found the experience to be much too overwhelming. If I ever want to be involved in a twelve-step program, I'll go line dancing at a country and western bar, thank you very much.

He's mean to my pets: I've had many pets over the years and have cared about them more than I cared for 99 percent of the men I dated. So whenever a guy pushed my cat aside or didn't pay attention to my dog and his furiously wagging tail, I decided to send him to the pound.

> **❝I was having sex with this guy and I guess my kitten was watching because when she saw his butt pumping away she got all excited and pounced on it. The guy screamed and pulled her claws out of his ass and threw my kitten across the room. I threw him away as well.❞**
>
> **—Elizabeth**

Clothes Make the Man . . . a Loser

True, you can't judge a book by its cover, but you certainly can judge a man by the clothes that cover him. What a man wears tells you a great deal about him and there are plenty of things he can put on that'll tell you he's a jerk. I'm not talking about a minor fashion faux pas like wearing white after Labor Day. I'm talking about giant garment goofs that are total deal breakers. Here are some no-noes that are bad enough to make even Ralph Lauren ralph.

He wears too much jewelry: To me, there's no bigger turnoff than a man who's bejeweled. Maybe it's because I think it's too feminine. Maybe it's because I think he's showing off. Or maybe it's because I'm just plain jealous because I want to be the one dripping in gold.

He wears way too many hair products: I like a guy with soft hair that I can run my fingers through. Who wants a guy who wears so many styling products that his hair is crunchy and gives you paper cuts all over your hands?

He wears his shirts unbuttoned to his navel: To be honest, I find the guy who wears his shirt like this to be even more repulsive than the look itself.

He wears jeans with ironed-in creases: Blech! Taking a perfectly good pair of sexy 501s and putting a crease down the front of the leg is like cutting a fold-over sandwich. All the goodness just runs right out of it.

He wears his pants pulled below his ass: A definite *Glamour Don't!* This look first became popular among convicts since inmates are forbidden to wear belts. I'm all for emulating fashion trends, but I prefer those that originate in Rome rather than Rikers.

He wears his pants hiked up to his nipple hair: These fashion victims deserve to be in prison. Unlike the previous look that was inspired by inmates, this look was inspired by the early-bird-special crowd. Because of their midsection paunch, they have to wear their pants hiked up or risk them falling down.

His Natural Habitat

If you had the advantage of seeing where your date lived in his natural habitat, consider yourself lucky. You've been given the gift of seeing a preview of how your life could be if you two were ever in a committed relationship. From the moment that you step foot into his pad, you'll be given an eyeful of clues (and maybe even a noseful of them, too) as to how your man behaves when left to his own devices. Some basic places that you should go to check out these clues are:

His movie collection: Sure, you can expect a lot of action-adventure films, but if there are more movies with titles like Ocean's Eleven Inches and The Passion of Christina, you may be in for trouble.

His refrigerator: Check out his fridge to see if it contains the four basic food groups or his own version of the food pyramid: beer, bologna, old take-out, and more beer. This means that if the two of you were to get together, you become "Chef Boy Am I Tired of Always Being the One to Cook in this Relationship." Just be warned that if his fridge is stocked with Marie Calendar potpies and Sara Lee dinners, you'll be taking over the cooking from these girls for the rest of your life.

His medicine cabinet: When you check out his medicine cabinet, don't look at it as invading his privacy; think of it as . . . well, I guess there's really no other way to look at it. But it is important to see if your date has any physical conditions or ailments that you should know about. You may not want to expose yourself to it if it's contagious or serious or just plain icky. When you think about it, you have the right to be informed about the medical condition of an animal that you take home from the pound. Why shouldn't you have the same rights when it comes to taking home a boyfriend?

In general, is his place clean or is it a breeding ground for penicillin?: If your date's a slob when he lives by himself, he's going to be a slob when he's living with you. Living with a slob can be especially difficult if you're a neat freak and are compulsive about having things your way, like folding your towels into thirds and making hospital corners on your bed. On the other hand, the same frustrations will apply if he's more of a Felix Unger and you're more like Oscar Madison. He may only be happy if the labels on the cans face front and his shirts are folded so well that they look like they're on sale at The Gap. When it comes to cleanliness, it's best if you are on the same page, or you'll forever be an Odd Couple.

Red Flag Alert

Now that you've examined every trait there is to know about your date, you need to take a look at any red flags that may have popped up during the evening. Although your first date with this guy was by far the most nerve-wracking of them all, it was also the most telling. Even though he may not have talked about many things besides himself, the few things that he did divulge are worth their weight in gold.

Here are some verbal red flags that he may have raised up the flagpole:

1. Did he tell you that he didn't see what the fuss was about Hitler?
2. Did he tell you that he's glad he "never done got more than a fifth grade education"?
3. Did he tell you that he just bought a pair of burial plots so that he can spend eternity next to his mother?
4. Did he tell you that he's finally accomplished his goal of drinking a can of beer through his nose?

5. Did he tell you that his hobby is collecting road kill?

6. Did he tell you that he speaks fluent Klingon?

Oftentimes, it's the things that your date *didn't* say that can be the most telling of them all. It's important to realize that many of his nonverbal communications can speak volumes about his true personality. You just need to know how to listen to the silence. Sure, there are obvious bad actions like stealing the silverware or grabbing your breast, but there are a host of other nonverbal cues that are far less subtle. Here are some of the nonverbal red flags that he may have raised:

1. Did he check his messages throughout the evening to see if his old girlfriend called?

2. Did he tap his fingers in boredom while you were telling him how your father passed away?

3. Did he slip his phone number into the waitress's bra?

4. Did he struggle to calculate that 15 percent tip?

5. Did he duck for cover whenever a policeman walked by?

Although most people would be bothered by at least a few of the red flags that I mentioned, sometimes a red flag is very subjective. For instance, I know that I detest driving in a car for a long period of time, so I'd be hesitant to start up a relationship with a guy who lived more than an hour away from where I live. To be honest, I'd even be reluctant to start up one if his parents lived more than an hour away from an airport hub. I'd go crazy every holiday and family occasion.

Maybe if you're a light sleeper you may reject a guy based purely on the state of his sinus congestion. I know that I wouldn't want to be up half the night listening to the irritating sound of construction noise going on at the next pillow.

And let's not forget the guys who have a passion for sports. It may sound like a little thing to you now, but if you like going out for Sunday brunch or, for that matter, going out during the day on Saturday and Sunday or at night on Monday and Thursday, then a sports lover isn't the guy for you. I'm forever amazed by the passion that guys have for certain teams when there's a really big game on . . . and there's always a big game.

As you can imagine, what exactly constitutes a red flag is subjective. Maybe you're a strict vegetarian and he's a hard-core meat eater. Maybe you're a die-hard Democrat and he's a devout Republican. Whatever the red flag may be, you need to determine which flags you can accept and which ones will be a constant and annoying thorn in your ass. When it comes to being involved with someone, you need to be picky. If you can manage to weed out a lot of the annoying traits now, you have a much better chance of growing a beautiful garden down the road that will last a lifetime.

The Test of Love

After reviewing and dissecting your first date, if you decided that he warrants a second one, you're still only halfway there. Now it's time for you to stand by helpless as your date decides if you're worth going out with again. But instead of going over the date with a fine-tooth comb and examining every detail like a Wall Street analyst, men have only one criteria they use when deciding whether they should ask you out again: whether or not you made their pee-pee tingle.

While your date is contemplating his decision, there's nothing you can do but sit back and wait for the results to come in. If this feeling brings on the sensation of déjà vu, you're right. For going out on a date is very much like another important event in your life: taking the SATs. In both instances, the test was excruciatingly difficult to endure and you're never really quite sure how you fared until you get the results back. You may think that you aced the exam, but then you get back scores only acceptable to a college that advertises in the back of *MAD* magazine.

Back when you took the SAT, you ran to the mailbox every day, waiting for the envelope to arrive that would forever change the course of your future. With a date, you sit by the phone every day waiting for that call to come in that will forever change the course of your future as well. When it comes to the scoring system of the SAT, we all know that a perfect score is a 1,600. But what are the possible scoring options when it comes to a date? As it turns out, there are three possible results:

Result Number One:
He Doesn't Call You at All
That phone call after a date is something that you always want to get. It doesn't matter if your date had the IQ of a ficus or was as exciting as canned meat, you still want that phone to ring so that you feel like you got a passing grade. If you don't get that phone call after a date, it can set you into a tailspin of self-pity that's far greater than any NASA disaster in U.S. history.

As much as being rejected by a loser can be extremely painful, being rejected by someone that you were interested in can be extremely frustrating. You know that finding someone that you feel potential with is as rare as finding a half-off Jimmy Choo sale. So you just sit there, waiting for a phone call that never comes. I'm sure that while you wait, you fight every instinct you have not to call him, and if it were me, I'd keep fighting. Just remind yourself that actions speak louder than words, and chances are that if you call him, the only words you'll hear from him will be those of rejection.

Result Number Two:
He Calls to Ask You Out, but You Don't
Want to Go Out with Him

A second option is that your date calls to ask you out again, but you don't have any desire to see him again. I know that many people would advise you to go out with him at least one more time before rejecting him, but I disagree. I think that men are like clothes in a department store. Once you try something on and you decide that you don't like it, why take it off and put it back on again? It doesn't somehow transform itself from a polyester muumuu into a Channel suit. Besides, if you go out with a bad date a second time, you're only prolonging the agony. And I don't mean his. If you thought that sitting through *Gigli* was dull, wait until you're on your second date with a guy who never interested you in the first place.

If a guy that you don't want to go out with again calls and asks you out, you are at an impossible fork in the road. You need to either agree to go out with him or to tell him that you're not interested. If you agree to go simply because you don't want to hurt his feelings, you're doomed to have an evening of torture. And then what? He's only going to assume that you like him and ask you out again. And this time if you reject him, it will hurt his feelings even more because you've gotten to know him better. So you agree to go out with him yet a third time to spare his feelings and this cycle will continue until you reject him, marry him, or move far, far away.

If you chose the other tong on the fork and decide to decline his offer for a second date, you may find that it's much easier said than done. The reason it's so hard to reject someone is that girls are taught at an early age to be nice and to spare other people's feelings. We're also taught to play with Barbies even though those stupid dolls can't stand up by themselves and are impossible to dress because the clothes get stuck in their thumbs. As you can see, many early lessons in life just lead to frustration.

Result Number Three:
He Likes You and He Does Ask You Out Again

Yes, I know that this scenario occurs as often as finding something good on TV opposite the Super Bowl. You get home from your date with a smile on your face and realize that, wonders of wonders, you actually had a great time. You found that your heart beat a bit faster and your deodorant worked a bit harder. And when you kissed your date good-night, you melted like the Wicked Witch of the East after Dorothy doused her with a bucket of water.

After you get home, you are filled with a renewed optimism and believe that maybe things really do work out in the end. Maybe, after all this waiting, it's finally your turn. You can't help but wonder if you just had your last first kiss!

But then you sit by the phone day after day waiting for it to ring. As each hour passes you feel your renewed spirit seep out of you like air from a balloon. You wonder what he can possibly be doing right now that's more important than calling you. You close your eyes and send off strong mental telepathic waves "Call me! Call me! Call me!" Then, just in case, you pick up the receiver to make sure that there's still a working dial tone. Yes, there is. But later, when you're running out the door, the phone rings, and, yes, it's him! Your cute little stud-muffin finally asks you out for a second date. You did it! You scored a 1,600 on the test of love! You passed with flying colors! Now comes the bad news! You have to go on another date!

The Second Interview

Granted, in some ways going out on a second date with a guy that you're interested in may be easier than going out on the first one, but this in no way means that your second date won't be nerve-wracking. In fact, you'll probably feel like you do before an important job interview. In both cases you really want to fill the position and you know that there's only one opening and 3 billion applicants whose only required qualification is a Y chromosome. You're also nervous because you don't really know exactly what kind of position is available. Is he only looking for part-time help or a year-round equal partner? And if you do get the position, will you work your ass off only to be traded in for a younger candidate?

Because of this, the second-date pressure can be strong. You know that the stakes are higher. You've passed the highly competitive first round and have not been cut from the long list of applicants. During the date, it's crucial to keep composed and not make any big mistakes. You have to walk the fine line of being yourself yet playing the game

“I went out on a second date with this guy that I thought could be the one. I was so excited that I laughed a bit too hard at his jokes and I would look at him a beat too long. The next day I got an e-mail from him telling me that he felt uncomfortable seeing me anymore because he could tell that I liked him.**”**

—Judith

right. You have to appear mysterious and unattainable while still being down to earth. You're like a schizophrenic in a cocktail dress. The pressure can be overwhelming. But remain calm and for heaven's sake, don't let him see you sweat! One false move and your date can toss your resume into the circular file and you're back pounding the pavement once again.

Things That Are Much Better to Do Without a Man

If for whatever reason, you don't get asked back for another interview, don't be glum, be glad! Don't fall head first into a pit of depression, but instead focus on all the wonderful things that you can do without a man by your side. Here are some of my personal favorites:

1. Go out for a shopping excursion for throw pillows. Men just never understand the beauty of a good throw pillow.

2. Visit a scrapbooking or craft store. Don't worry what you look like; you're guaranteed not to see even one man there.

3. Go to the annual Gilmore garlic festival. This way you can gorge yourself on everything from garlic chicken to garlic ice cream and not have to worry about stinky breath.

4. Rent a sexy movie that doesn't entail any girl on girl action.

5. Go out for high tea. There is nothing more dignified or girly than going out for tea. There's just something about that steamy beverage and crustless points of bread that make you hold your pinky high.

chapter seven

to insanity and beyond!

Once a guy asks you out on a couple of dates you can pretty much assume that he likes you. And, if you say yes to his request, you can pretty much assume that you like him, too. But as you know, things are anything but smooth sailing from here on in. Sure, after a few dates there's far less chance that a big ball will drop. By now you already know if your date has kids, a pierced tongue, or hasn't held down a job since parachute pants were all the rage.

But even though there may be many more chapters in your relationship, these next dating hurdles can be the most emotionally taxing of them all. Sure, there may be a pot of gold at the end of the rainbow, but, like the rainbow, your relationship is very unstable. Just one of any number of dating disasters can turn those brilliant colors into gray.

Don't get me wrong. I'm not saying that you shouldn't be thrilled just to get this far. But you'd think that once the first date crap is over that the cards would just fall into place. But no. The dating gods aren't that kind. They must get a giggle out of kicking you in the Achilles' heel of love over and over again.

Limbo Guy

There's a whole gray area of dating. It's when you've gone out with a guy a couple of times but he's still far from being your boyfriend. During this gray area, you know that you both like each other, but it's still very early on in the relationship. Because of this, you can't get him to do the things that a true boyfriend would do. It's during this temporary stage, I refer to that special someone as "Limbo Guy."

Having a Limbo Guy in your life is sort of the nowhere zone of couple-hood. It's a place that's devoid of any rules and regulations that are automatically in effect when you are part of a twosome. Although this stage can be difficult for you, it's just the way Limbo Guy likes it.

When you've dated a man long enough to call him your boyfriend, he pretty much knows what's expected of him. He knows that he's required to call you when you're sick and to take you out on your birthday. He understands that he'll be the one to drive you to the mechanic when your car won't start and to pretend to like your mother during family functions. And he's fully aware that it's his job to sit bored for hours on end holding your handbag while the two of you go shopping.

But the rules for Limbo Guy are not as clear-cut. Limbo Guy doesn't have to clean up after himself when he makes a mess at your place. He doesn't have to share his popcorn with you at the movies. Hell, he can even see other women if he wants to. He can be thoughtless and rude at any given moment and get away with it because he knows that it's much too early in your relationship to have any big battles or get into the exclusivity talk. In fact, being a Limbo Guy is the ideal situation for a man. He's like a witness with immunity and he's in hog heaven.

But this free-range stage of a relationship has the opposite effect on us women. We find being in this no-confrontation phase to be extremely frustrating and stand helpless to do anything to change it. It's like being in New York in August and not wanting frizzy hair. The reason that this stage is so aggravating is that we don't like gray areas. We like to have things a certain way. We like our shoes to match our bag and our dressing on the side. We like our bacon crispy and our laundry to smell April fresh.

We also know that if we push our guy to become our boyfriend before he's ready, he'll run faster than cheap pantyhose. Sure, down the road we can tell our guy what bothers us and what things we'd like to change. But at this point, we must keep our lips sealed. And as you know, keeping our feelings inside makes us feel like we're going to explode. So we choose to say nothing. Instead, we focus on the fact that it won't be long until the tables are turned and we can blab away about our feelings while the men stand by in silence.

Temporary Insanity

There is nothing quite like those few first tender months of a new relationship. You like him, you know he likes you, and life as you know it is like one wild ride. An advantage of being in those first crazed emotional weeks of a new romance is that you can actually commit murder and no jury of your peers (which would consist of a dozen other crazed women) would ever convict you. These women know firsthand the highs and lows that dating a guy that you're actually interested in can bring. They're on the same emotional roller coaster ride as you are and know exactly how nauseating it can be.

The highs of this roller coaster are more exhilarating than any white-knuckler you've ever experienced. Oh, the exhilaration you feel when your special guy takes your hand in his as you walk down the street. Or the heart-stopping elation when he sends you flowers for the first time or calls you just to hear the sound of your voice. You think about him all the time and get that warm ball of excitement in the pit of your stomach when you do. If Disneyland could ever create a roller coaster that duplicates these highs, it really would be the happiest place on earth. I'd call it the "Nothing Else in the World but Him Does Matterhorn."

But unfortunately, what comes up must also come down and these highs can come crashing back to Earth at a moments notice. It could be when he forgets it's your birthday even though you told him about it just a few days before. It could be when he ends your date early so he can go play poker with the boys. Or it could be when you surprised him at work only to be surprised yourself when you find him in the coffee room heating up another woman's decaf.

When you're on this turbulent ride, you realize who your true friends really are, and who's just been hanging around to take advantage of your employee discount. That's because

❝I was so obsessed with my boyfriend when we first started going out. I'd save every message he left on my machine and I'd keep every note he wrote. I couldn't even throw away the trash in the bathroom because it had Kleenex that he used to blow his nose in. It was like always having a part of him still here. Man, I was so sick.❞

—Jaime

you're not sitting alone on that roller coaster; you're drag-
ging your friends right along with you for the ride. Their
safety bar is locked tightly in place beside you and they're in
for their own share of abuse. You ask their opinion on what
you should wear before each date to see if it's too Carmen
Electra or too Carmen Miranda. You call them afterward no
matter what the time to tell them about it. You force them
to listen to every message he's ever left on your answering
machine over and over again to decipher what he meant by
saying, "Hi, Babe."

The reason that you've become such a mental wreck during these early stages of a relationship is that you can't seem
to get this man off your mind. You think about him all
the time and obsess about every little thing he says or does.
"Why hasn't he tried to get me into bed yet?" "Is there a reason why he hasn't introduced me to his friends yet?" "Is that
spot on his neck really a bug bite or did someone give him
a hickey?" You try not to think about him, but he's stuck
in your head like a subdural hematoma that's just below the
inner layer of the dura mater. (I picked up a few things from
watching *ER*.)

You're like an addict in search of a fix. You drive by the
place where you first kissed, trying to recapture the thrill.
You call his home machine when you know he's at the office
just so you can hear the sound of his voice. You go to a psy-
chic so that you can hear if he's the one you've been looking for your whole life. You struggle to keep yourself busy
in between his phone calls, all the while wondering why
he isn't calling you. It's enough to drive any sane woman
insane!

I wish I had some suggestions on how to calm yourself
down. I'd tell you to drink a cup of chamomile tea, but

that'd be like taking baby aspirin to ease the pains of child-birth. What you really need is some hard-core help that only chocolate cake and double fudge brownies can provide. To ease the stress of this addictive time, you could go to the Betty Ford Clinic, but I think you'd find more comfort from another Betty: Betty Crocker.

Push-Me-Pull-You Dance of Intimacy

Human nature is a very strange thing. It makes us desire something that we can't have. It makes us come together in times of hardship. And it makes us pull away from some-one we care about when that person comes closer to us. At least emotionally it does. When it comes to being in a rela-tionship, we're all like that two-headed mutant llama from Dr. Doolittle, and when one side of that Push-Me-Pull-You moves closer, the other side backs away.

We've all seen that llama rear both its ugly heads in at least one of our past relationships. You've felt your new potential love get closer to you, and you're aware that his feelings toward you have deepened and his dependency on you has bloomed. You start to feel like you have someone in your life who really cares about you, and then WHAMO! He takes a giant emotional step backwards. He stops calling as often, and when he does, he sounds much more aloof and distant. He cancels plans for the weekend because some sudden and mysterious "friend" comes in from out of town. He doesn't want to cuddle on the sofa anymore but instead chooses to sit in the armchair on the other side of the room. Suddenly and without any warning, your man became emotionally distant. It's as if you are playing a game of relationship Chutes and Ladders and he just landed on a giant chute that took him all the way back to square one. When something like this happens, your first reaction is to hold on to him even tighter. You dig those long, Sally Hansen Hard as Nails deep into him and hold on for dear life. You call him all the time to ask him if he wants to get together. You drop by his place with a burger from the place that he took you on your first date. You try anything you can to ignite sparks into a dying flame. You can't stand the thought of your new guy pulling away, so you panic and cling to him like cheese on a cold pizza. The problem is that the more you hold on, the more he tries to push you away.

Although there is always that chance that he's becoming disinterested in the relationship, there's a far greater chance that he's backing away because of the one flaw that all men have: they're stupid. They look strong and self-confident on the outside, but on the inside, they're nothing but Twinkie cream. They try as hard as they can to cover up this fact, but when they meet someone they care about, they let down their defenses. But once they let you in enough to see their vulnerability, they panic and act tough and nonchalant. And that's when you feel them start backing away.

So if holding on tighter doesn't solve the problem, what will? Do you have to sit by helpless as you watch your dreamboat sail off to sea? Of course not. You just need to use the magic of the same Push-Me-Pull-You strategy. If you can muster up the strength to take one giant step backwards yourself, your man will likely take one step closer toward you. From now on, if he leaves a message on your answering machine, don't call him back right away the way you used to. If he does ask you out, tell him that you have plans. As soon as he sees that you're slipping away, he'll become the cold cheese and hold on to you, and you can smile once again.

Don't be surprised if your relationship goes through this Push-Me-Pull-You dance of intimacy several times in your relationship. He just may need more time to feel secure so that he doesn't feel the need to flee. And if you can recognize the warning signs, you won't make the crucial mistake of smothering him when what he really needs is a little space. Just remember that a guy needs to establish some trust in you before he can show you his Twinkie cream.

You Are What You Hate

You've hated them all your life. They're the kind of women who drop their girlfriends whenever they have a man in their lives. They cancel plans on you at the last minute. They monopolize the conversation about every little detail about their heartthrob. You've called these women desperate and shallow and even harsher words that I can't mention if I want this book to sell at Wal-Mart. Well, now you can call them by another name: (Insert Your Name Here), because you, my friend, have become one of them.

Yes, now that you have someone in your life, you've hit rock bottom and have become one of those women that you swore that you'd never become. I understand why you didn't see it coming. The transformation happened gradually. For the first few weeks you weren't even aware there were any changes. But now they're in full force and you notice a powerful change in your behavior.

To begin with, you're losing your sense of self. Before you began this relationship you were an independent woman with your own likes and dislikes. But now it seems that you're taking on more of your man's interests than your own. If he likes to garden, you're knee-deep in manure. If he likes to fish, you're out on the lake sticking a hook through a live minnow. If he likes old movies, you put aside your love of Hugh Grant for his love of Cary Grant. Although you tell yourself that you're just expanding your interests, you know deep down that what you're really doing is just taking on his.

There are other signs that will tell you if you're becoming one of "those girls." Here are some things to look out for that could mean you, too, have become transformed:

1. You ramble on and on about your new love interest to the checkout girl, the 4-1-1 operator, or anyone else who will listen.
2. You forget to call your sister when she had a fibroid removed because you were too obsessed with what to wear to your new guy's business dinner.
3. None of your girlfriends call you anymore because they're sick of hearing about the bladder infection that you got from having so much sex.

You may have come to the conclusion that you've become one of "those girls" on your own, or maybe your neglected friends teamed up and had an intervention. Whichever way it happened, you now understand that you've crossed the bridge over to the land of self-centeredness. You've hurt your friends and neglected your family and it's time to take a U-turn back to the way things were. But you have to wonder, if it's so wrong, why does it feel so right?

Dating Miscarriage

In many ways being in a relationship is like being pregnant. Some people fall into the situation quite easily, needing only a couple of glasses of wine and a night of reruns. For others, it means years of struggle and spending thousands of dollars on professional services. But no matter how you wind up in the situation, both dating and pregnancy have one thing in common: They can end in an instant without any warning signs whatsoever.

The reason for this is because a new relationship, like a new life form, is very fragile during the first few months. There are many connections that have to be made and crucial tests that need to be passed. In the case of a fetus, cells have to divide at the precise time. The egg has to attach itself well to the womb. And the woman's hormones have to increase so she'll have strong enough mood swings to yell at her hubby. If any of these steps are done incorrectly or in the wrong time frame, your dream cannot survive.

With dating, the same situation is true. At any given moment, a wrench can be thrown into the fires of love and melt it down like a birthday candle in a kiln. Like pregnancy, there can be many reasons for its demise and you never see it coming. All you know is that one day, it's over. He stops calling and if you call him, he gives you the cold shoulder. Maybe he had the courage to tell you it was over face to face or maybe he was weak and sent the message by e-mail. And now, like with pregnancy, your dreams have died too.

Chances are, you weren't even aware that your relationship had any problems. In most instances of a dating miscarriage there were no warning signs. You thought that the two of you were building a foundation that was healthy and

> **“**I went out with this guy once and everything seemed great. But then he stopped calling and I couldn't stop crying. I later found out that he dumped me because he saw a photograph of my mother, who's quite heavy. He believed in that saying, like all men do, that a woman will grow up to look like her mother. After I heard that, I stopped crying and counted my blessings.**”**
>
> —Alexis

strong. You were excited about your future together and even shared your good news with your family and close friends. And then suddenly, without any cramping or bleeding or confrontations of any kind, it's over.

Of course you blame yourself. You try to pinpoint the moment things went amiss. Was it the time you ordered the expensive crab cakes instead of just going with the burger? Maybe he freaked when you held your neighbor's newborn and kept saying how cute he was. Or maybe it was when the two of you passed by a jewelry store and you stopped to look at the diamond rings. You rewind your relationship, desperately seeking clues. But like Paris Hilton's success, it may forever remain a mystery.

Chances are that you may never know that truth about what really happened. At this tender and delicate stage of your relationship, it could never handle the stress of an open confrontation. At his point, there's not much you can do but accept that your dream is dead. You sadly tell your friends and family that it's over and they all give you their sympathies. There's really not much they can say. All you can do is accept it and hope that next time, the outcome will be better. Maybe next time you'll get that miracle that you truly deserve, and you'll find someone to take care of, and cook for, and clean up after . . . for the rest of your life.

Cheater Pants

Men cheat. They cheat in business (think of the corporate heads of Enron). They cheat in politics (think of the Watergate conspiracy). And they cheat in love (think of the entire male population of the human race). Many social scientists agree that one big reason men stray is that it's ingrained into their DNA. Mother Nature is one smart mama and her main goal is to keep her species alive. She knows that one good way of doing this is for her boys to spread their seeds wherever they see young, nubile soil. By doing so, not only will it continue the species, but the lives that are created will carry on less genetic defects as well. Many defects require that both mother and father are carriers, but when the defect is only carried by one parent, it will not be passed onto the child. Mama Nature must have aced biology.

I know many relationships that ended in cheating. I was a victim of this evolutionary condition as well. I'm a very gullible person. I don't notice a lot of signs, and I easily rationalize away the ones I do notice. Although this makes me an easy target for a surprise party, it makes me an easy target for being cheated on as well.

I had been dating a man for a while and had gotten to know him pretty well. Once when I was at his house, I noticed that his VCR was missing. When I asked him about it he said that it broke and that he took it in to be fixed. Hmmm, something didn't compute. This guy was so lazy that he'd throw his dirty dishes away rather than wash them. There was no way that he would go to all the trouble to get his VCR fixed. That's when time stood still and I was mentally bombarded by other inconsistencies, like how he'd been working late and that he'd been taking an awful lot of showers. Hmmm, after a dozen pebbles, I was finally hit in the head by that brick.

When I asked him where he took his VCR to be fixed and what they said the problem was, he confessed that he had given his VCR to someone else. When I pushed even further, he admitted that this was someone that he had been seeing. Now it was time to push even more and push that creep right out of my life. I'm not sure if I was more upset that he was cheating on me or that he gave some bimbo a VCR when he wouldn't even loan me his Aero bed when a friend of mine came to visit.

If you suspect that a guy you're seeing is seeing someone else, there are some basic clues to look out for, like if he's been less affectionate, joins a gym, and buys new clothes. But there are other telltale signs as well, like the following:

1. He writes you a note on hotel stationery.
2. Your waitress pours coffee in his lap and says, "I can't believe you brought her here!"
3. He uses a pair of panties as a car chamois after you find it in his glove compartment.
4. In the heat of passion, he calls you another woman's name.
5. In the heat of passion, he calls you another guy's name.

If you answered yes to one or more of the preceding questions, then your gut instincts may be right and he may indeed be a Mr. Cheater Pants. If you can, probe deeper. Look at his credit card bill. Check out the past callers on his cell phone. Browse through his list of deleted e-mail. Most men do a poor job of covering up their tracks if they cheat. You may think that there's a part of them that wants to be caught. I just think that they're lazy. But before you explore any deeper, make sure that you're prepared to find out the truth.

I hope that you never have to experience the kind of pain that cheating can inflict. It's a pain that cuts so deep that it can influence you for the rest of your life. Your self-confidence will be destroyed, and no matter who you're with from then on out, you'll be far less likely to trust him. You'll forever question where he's going or who he's going with. Even though his temptation to cheat may be ingrained in his DNA, that doesn't give him license to give in to this temptation. We women fight off temptation every time we walk past a Cinnabon. Sure, the need may be in his genes, but if a man cheats on me ever again, I'm gonna cut off what's inside his jeans.

I Love You, You Love Me Not

There's not one woman out there who hasn't felt the agony of being rejected. We've all been hurt when it comes to matters of the heart and it's a pain that we've felt since we were very young. The first time I felt rejection was when I had my first girl crush on Michelle Kagen back in kindergarten. She had long blond hair and a nose covered in freckles and she could curl her tongue into the shape of a clover. I wanted to be friends with her so badly that it made my baby teeth hurt. And for a while, we were. That is until that new girl came to school. Her name was Tammy Greene and once she and Michelle met,

I was history. From then on I'd see them sharing the same mat during naptime and nibbling from the same jar of paste. My itty-bitty heart broke in two. Why didn't Michelle want to sit next to me? I shared my blocks with her. I gave her my pudding cup. Why didn't she like me anymore?

Being rejected is the female equivalent to being kicked in the balls. It's a pain that's worse than anything else life has to offer. Well, maybe that's not true. Having a loved one die can be far more devastating. Or being diagnosed with a terminal illness would no doubt be worse. Or, for that matter, having a full-body craving for a glazed buttermilk doughnut only to find out that the skinny woman who can eat anything she wants without getting fat has taken the last one. Where was I? . . . oh yeah, rejection.

There are many theories that advise you how long you can expect this pain to last. One theory is that it takes half of the time you were with someone to get over that person. Another one says that you'll get over him as soon as you find someone else to take his place. Personally, I'd subscribe to any theories that involve chocolate. To tell you the truth, I don't think that any theory is true in every case because I believe some guys you simply never do get over. I know that there are a handful of men who have burrowed into my heart and will remain there forever. I know that if I were to ever run into one of these ex loves who dumped me, I'd duck for cover no matter how much time passed.

One factor that affects your pain level is if you left the relationship having the upper hand. Any woman who's been dumped before knows about the importance of having "hand" and she also knows how to get it. She can sniff out a guy who's about to break up with her like a German Shepherd zoning in on a suitcase full of cocaine. She's been there before and has learned to recognize the signs. The crowded restaurant. His double vodka. The meal he's left untouched. She knows that if she sees these signs, sometime during dessert he'll say, "We have to talk." Then she must immediately follow it up with, "Yes, I know. I think we should break up." As they say, the best defense is a good offense, and if done correctly, the relationship will end with you getting "hand" and him feeling like he's been given the boot.

But even if you do have hand, you still can expect to feel pain for a while. Although nothing will take it away, I do have some ideas about how to soften the blow:

1. Change the preset dials on your radio to Rush Limbaugh, Howard Stern, or any talk radio program. If you hear just one love song during your healing process, you'll shed so many tears that your appendages will turn to dust.
2. Pamper yourself. Buy yourself treats like good face cream and outrageously expensive coffee. Better yet, if he has a charge account at a certain store, let him buy it for you.
3. Shop! Chances are if your heart's been broken you've dropped a couple of pounds due to depression. In fact, there's no better or faster way to lose weight short of giving birth. Take advantage of your new smaller dress size by buying lots of new dresses. Not only will it make you feel pretty, but the ogles you'll get from men can boost your low self-image.

I wish I had an easy fix for this pain. I could try telling you that you're not alone and that we've all been through it at one time or another. I could rehash the phrase that time cures all. I could say that they're having a two-for-one sale on Ding Dongs. But we both know that there's nothing I can say that will take the heartache away (although the Ding Dongs really do seem to numb the pain for a while).

The Best Part about Being Single Again

Although there are many things that you'll miss now that you don't have a man in your life, you need to focus on the positives. There were many things that you didn't feel comfortable doing before that you can finally start doing again. Here are some of the things that may just make it worth having one less bell to answer, one less egg to fry:

- You can eat a whole pint of ice cream from the container and have nobody judge you.
- You don't have to pretend to like sports.
- You don't have to see movies that star Jackie Chan.
- You don't have to listen to snoring.
- You can watch the entire *Sex and the City* marathon because you now control the remote control.
- You don't have to read *Time* magazine anymore and can go back to buying your favorite tabloids.
- You can squeeze your blackheads anytime you want.
- You can dress nice without anyone expecting you to have sex with him.

chapter eight

the sexual revulsion

If I were to have written this book before 1960, I wouldn't have even included a section on dating sex. Actually I wouldn't have included any sections at all since I was only a gleam in my father's eye back then and would have had limited typing skills. Before about 1960, the rule of that time was "good girls don't have sex before marriage." Period. But the turbulent sixties brought forth many changes to our culture, like sex, drugs, rock 'n' roll, and the introduction of that cute yellow round guy that said, "Have a nice day." Because of the newfound sexual revolution, what was once considered abnormal is now considered the norm, and sex is now as much a part of dating as whitener is a part of toothpaste.

As we discussed earlier in the book, there are some emotional dangers that you face when deciding whether or not to sleep with someone for the first time. But even more important than the emotional dangers of having sex are the physical ones that weren't even an issue in decades past. There are now a bevy of sexually transmitted diseases to worry about from herpes to AIDS. It seems that infected bodily fluids are now classified as a concealed weapon, and you're forced to have an awkward talk before he conceals his weapon inside of you. You need to ask the guy you're thinking of having sex with if he's been tested for AIDS, if he's ever used intravenous drugs, if he's ever had sexual relations with a man, and how many sexual partners he's had. As you can imagine, an interview such as this can certainly take the air out of his tire. Because of this, the conversation needs to be carefully timed. If you question him too early, it can kill the spontaneity. If you question him too late, it can kill the mood. And if you don't question him at all, it can kill you.

As if that's not enough reason to become celibate, there's also the issue of pregnancy to deal with. These days you have to be a good little girl scout and come prepared. If the condom is your prophylactic of choice, which one should you buy? If you use a diaphragm, that means carrying a small pharmacy inside your purse. You'll need the diaphragm, its case, the goop inserter in case you want seconds, and the goop itself. If you're on the pill, the man you're with may deduce that you use it because you sleep around. You also have to worry about the side effects of the pill. When I was on it, I remember reading the warning label about the possible weight gain, depression, skin problems, and gum inflammation. No wonder the pill is so effective. If you use it, no one will want to have sex with you. As you can see, even the most causal sex is anything but casual.

But even with all the problems that dating sex can bring, at some point in your relationship, you will probably decide that you want a romp in the hay. Maybe you've spent enough time with a certain man that you trust him enough to give yourself to him. Maybe you've had one too many dirty martinis and you feel like being dirty yourself. Or maybe you haven't had sex for so long that your labia are starting to grow together. Whatever the reason, whenever you feel that the time is right, get ready to have dating sex. But let me warn you: Whoever created the expression "there's no such thing as bad sex," has never experienced dating sex. Here are just a few of the things that you can expect.

Kissing Catastrophes

I'm sure we all can agree that if the man that we're seeing is a good kisser, we can forgive him for a multitude of other flaws. Kissing is one of the most personal and erotic aspects of a sexual relationship and when it is not good, it is a definite deal breaker for me. Kissing is to sex what a starter is to a car and if it fails, it's much harder to get your engine running. If you ever find yourself in possession of a guy who excels in the kissing department, hold on to him as tightly as you would the secret behind the Mrs. Fields cookie recipe.

But if you have yourself a guy with lousy lip service, you're in for big trouble. Making out with a bad kisser is like eating a bad clam. It's vile and retched and leaves a bad taste in your mouth that can last a lifetime. I still think back on some of the bad clams that I've kissed and I'm suddenly filled with disgust. You'd think that a guy who's a bad kisser would come with a warning label. Other women must have sampled his goods and it should be their civic responsibility to report them to the authorities as they would a crime or a bad diet pill. Don't expect a man to let you in on his lack of lip luster. All men seem to take great pride in their oral communication and are completely oblivious to the fact that they repel women.

Just as there is more than one way to skin a cat (an expression I really don't want to know the history behind), there is also more than one way to be a bad kisser. Here are some of the most common smooching sins:

Bad breath: If a guy suffers from bad breath, you, my friend, will suffer right along with him. You'll find that your eyes will water more than when you're peeling an onion.

The harpoonist: In this case, a guy uses his tongue to search for . . . God only knows what the hell he's searching for. All I know is that if you find a way to strap a camera to the end of his tongue he could give you a colonoscopy while the two of you are making out.

The clam mouth: This is a guy who likes to rest his tongue on yours as if it were a clam. To me, this is the epitome of laziness. Even the guy's tongue is a couch potato.

The sucker: He likes to suck on your lips and tongue. Get a tootsie pop and leave me the hell alone!

The licker: He's similar to the sucker but he likes to use your mouth area as if it were a giant postage stamp.

The dentist: This is a guy who gives you a dental cleaning with every kiss because he licks your teeth and gums. Although he might be preventing tarter buildup, he's also preventing a relationship with me.

The nipper: This is a guy who attacks your lips like a boarder collie herding sheep. He literally nips at your lips until they're bloody and sore.

The repressed: Some men don't even bother to open their mouth when they kiss. It reminds me of how movie stars kissed on the big screen back in the chaste 1940s. These guys probably have sex with one foot still on the floor as well.

If you really like a guy except for his lack of tongue titillation, there may be hope. To some degree a bad kisser can be taught to mend his ways. With some redirection and nonverbal communication, there is a chance that he won't be so repulsive. But don't expect miracles. A bad kisser can never be made to be great. He can only be made to be less revolting. When it comes to kissing, you either got it or you don't.

Foreplay Schmoreplay

When I think of what men and women want in bed, I think of that old nursery rhyme, Jack Sprat. Remember, "Jack Sprat could eat no fat. His wife could eat no lean. So between the two of them they licked the platter clean." When you think about it, the sexual appetite of men and women differs to this same degree. We both like completely opposite things and this difference is never quite as apparent as when it comes to what gets us hot.

For women to get in the mood, we need a lot of hand holding and kissing. We thrive on being caressed and nuzzled. If a man wants to go to bed with us that night, he needs to start getting us ready first thing that morning. He needs to call for no apparent reason and bring us a little surprise when he picks us up. He needs to compliment us frequently and gaze deeply into our eyes.

Men, on the other hand, don't require any foreplay in order to get aroused. In fact, they think of it as a big waste of time. They can get ready at the drop of a hat, morning, noon, or night. All that they require to get in the mood is a quick glimpse of you unloading the dishwasher or even simply putting a coin into a vending machine.

We can't really get upset at men for feeling this way. Well, of course we can, and we do it quite often, but it never seems to change anything. I find the most insensitive part of the whole matter is that they treat their cars better than they treat their women. I guarantee that if it's a cold morning, they take ample time to warm up their vehicle before taking it out on the road. But no matter how cold *our* motor is, they simply hold onto their stick shift and put it into high gear.

I think the problem all boils down to porn (as do many other problems in a relationship). Women in porn movies are always ready to go whenever the pizza man, delivery boy, or fireman drops by. And since porn is the building block of men's sexual education, they believe that all women act in this manner, or at least they really wish that they would.

Men just don't have the patience that we women do. They thrive on immediate gratification. They don't understand the pleasure of savoring an appetizer before the main course. They don't like taking the longer, more scenic route. When they want something, they want it now and anything that delays their gratification is seen only as a waste of time.

Maybe the way to release our pent-up frustrations is to create our own form of brothel. But instead of providing the same sexual services that appeal to men, like various forms of intercourse, ours would provide pleasures like spooning, back rubs, and nibbles to the nape of the neck. Now that's something I think could really catch on!

Funky-Looking Genitals

Let's face it. Male genitalia aren't very attractive. I prefer my bodily organs to be on the inside, and this organ is no exception. It's nothing personal. I'd feel the same way if a guy's spleen were dangling out of his belly button. To make matters even worse, even though all men have the same parts, not all of these body parts are created equal.

Take a guy's testicles for instance. I guarantee that those two dangly little doohickeys are responsible for half of the lesbian population. They're lumpy and hairy and have the consistency and appearance of a rotten fig. There are tremendous size variations among them as well. Some men have small ones while others are quite large. It's as if they've sprayed Miracle Grow on those puppies each spring. Some are close to the body while others flap around like turkey waddles.

As if the looks of the things aren't bad enough, they're given really horrible names as well. Names like "testes," "ball sack," and "scrotum." There's just nothing erotic about these words and saying them seems to stick in your mouth as much as they do.

Then there's the penis itself to deal with. I'll grant you that it's fascinating to watch it go through its metamorphosis and change from a caterpillar to a cucumber. It reminds me of those inflatable life rafts that expand after their string has been pulled. And of course, there's the whole issue of the foreskin on the penis to deal with. Personally I'm glad that circumcisions have become so commonplace nowadays. I've actually never seen an uncircumcised penis in real life and I'm glad that I never have. I imagine that it looks something like a sharpie, and I think I'd have about as much desire to touch it as I do a raw chicken.

The Two-Pump Chump

Once in a while you'll be with a man who takes as long to finish having sex as it does to blow his nose. If you haven't been with a guy who suffers from this, imagine someone offering you a warm chocolate chip cookie and then yanking it away just before you can sink your teeth into it. As you can imagine, you're left feeling frustrated and unsatisfied. When it comes to sex and chewy baked goods, a girl does not like to be denied.

If, after this happens, the man you're with apologizes profusely and tells you that this kind of thing has never happened to him before, you can easily rationalize it away. You can tell yourself that it's probably been awhile since he's had sex or that you simply turned him on with the intensity of stadium lights. We women always have a good rationalization for things, which is why we have so many shoes.

But if this occurrence happens again, it becomes more difficult to sweep under the proverbial rug. You realize that this must be a recurring problem. When this is the case,

66 Before I slept with this guy for the first time, I went in his

bathroom to change and noticed a bunch of dirty Q-tips in

his trashcan. I couldn't figure out what they were from until I

discovered that the guy wasn't circumcised. I guess that's how

he has to clean himself in there. Ewwww!99

—Lizzy

there are things that you can do to try to slow things down. You can use sexual-buzz-killer words like "your mother," "vaginal discharge," and, of course, "tampon." But if he still huffs and puffs and blows away the record for the fastest orgasm, you have to accept the fact that you're with a two-Pump Chump.

The Energizer Bunny

On the other end of this sexual spectrum is the guy who can last longer than the Energizer bunny. He can keep going and going until the cows come home, and the tractor is put in the shed, and the supper dishes have been dried and stacked clean, and tomorrows biscuit dough has been kneaded and is in the oven to rise, and . . . well, you get the idea.

I'm sure the men in these sexual marathons actually believe that they're giving you great pleasure. What they don't realize is what they're really doing is giving you internal rug burn. As these guys rub you raw, they imagine that you're drifting away on a sea of sexual fantasies, when in truth what you're really doing is killing time imagining what the ceiling would look like painted eggshell.

If you're with an Energizer bunny there's really only one thing to do. Take out his batteries. You need to exhaust this guy of his power supply. Feed him turkey before he goes to bed at night so that the tryptophan makes him drowsy. Tell him to go for a run before turning in that night. Or, of course, just fake it. Get it over with so you can finally roll over and get some sleep. If none of these ideas work, call out another guy's name. Nothing will stop him dead in his tracks faster than that.

Men need to realize that having sex is not like running a marathon. It should provide intimacy, not the need for blister medication. It should give us a feeling of closeness, not calluses. So if your fella grabs you and tells you that he wants to make love to you all night long, be afraid. Be very afraid.

Mr. Too Big

I'm sure you've heard the expression "The bigger the better." And while it may be true for the size of apple martinis, it certainly isn't the case when it comes to the size of male genitalia. Since the average length of the vagina is only about five inches and the size of some men's penises can hit the double digits, you understand why the old myth that you've always believed may not be true. Despite what you've heard, there really are instances where you could have too much of a good thing.

Having sex with a man that's been endowed with an exceptionally large penis is like having sex for the first time. In both cases you know that it will involve pain and bleeding, and in both cases, you'll just want to get the whole thing over with as quickly as possible. When you come right down to it, we women are like horny little Goldilocks forever in search of a penis that's just the right size. And a penis that's too big does not make for a happy ending.

Although being a "big man on campus" gave these guys plenty of pride back in the junior high school shower rooms, it may now be giving them some problems. These supersized jocks are well aware that their dip stick can damage your oil tank because they've seen firsthand the kind of physical

> **"**I dated this guy for a while named Steve, but some of his friend's occasionally referred to him by the nickname 'Redwood.' I always wondered why they called him that, but when we finally had sex, it all became abundantly clear.**"**
>
> —Annie

discomfort being physical can bring. Because of this, Mr. Too Big may warn you before going in, like a doctor does before giving you an injection. He'll tell you that you may let out some moans and groans during lovemaking that have nothing to do with pleasure. He may even suggest having sex in certain positions that might lessen the discomfort. But unless you're a contortionist with the Cirque du Soleil, you may have some trouble achieving these positions.

Oftentimes a well-endowed man has to restrict himself to only partial penetration. Although this may give you great relief, it gives him nothing but frustration. It's like being blessed with an amazing voice and only being allowed to hum. So if you date a guy who turns out to be a giant among men, be warned. You may need a few apple martinis yourself to relax yourself enough before the big, and I mean big, event.

Physical Shortcomings

Men are brave. They watch scary movies without having to peek through their fingers. They go after intruders with only a bat in hand to defend themselves. But no matter how brave they appear to be, they're all deathly afraid of three simple words: size does matter. It seems that men think the size of their penis coincides with their sexual competence and women are like Olympic judges who are all looking for a perfect ten.

There are actually two forces at work when it comes to the size of a man's penis: length and girth. If only one of these factors is affected, you may be okay. But if he is lacking in both of these areas, you can expect to arrive in Frustration City very soon. For those of you who have been with a Wee Willie Winky before, you know firsthand the frustration I'm talking about. Here you've been building up sexual tension for weeks imagining how wonderful it will be when the two of you finally get together. You're sure that all you'll see is fireworks. But then when the two of you finally become one, the only thing that goes through your mind is that song "Is That All There Is My Friend?"

There's another inherent problem with a Johnson that's anything but Magic, and this one tends to be quite embarrassing. Since this guy's hot dog can't quite fill your bun, he pumps a lot of air inside of you while you're having sex, which comes out of you afterward as one large vaginal fart. You lie there mortified, when he's the one that should be embarrassed since he has a dick the size of an o.b. tampon.

Although in most cases you never know the size of his penis until he gets undressed, there are a couple of ways to stalk out a man with this physical shortcoming. One way is to check out the size of a guy's hands and the size of his shoes. The second is to check out the kind of car that he drives. Usually the more power *it* has, the less pecker *he* has.

I know that having sex with a guy who has a small dick isn't the worst thing in the world. But doing so gives you the same feeling you get after you've eaten a plate of spa food. In both cases you're never filled up and the experience leaves you unsatisfied and wanting more. I know that some good things in life come in small packages, but if a guy has a small package, you won't be coming at all.

Boys Can Be Kinky Boys

Here you are in the arms of your big, strong man ready for some gentle lovemaking, but instead of intimacy, all you get is shock. For even if your sex life starts off on a good note, that doesn't mean that it won't end up sounding like an American Idol reject after a bit of time. That's because men have a tendency to be kinky and want to perform some sexual acts that are illegal in forty-two states. But men have learned that they can't show this kinky side too early on in a relationship. If they did, women would want to run away as fast as men do when they're confronted with that "Where is this relationship headed?" conversation.

You may be thinking that you're lucky and that you've escaped this problem. So far the only deviant request that he's made is wanting to eat crackers in bed despite the risk of crumbs. But just because he's been content doing the missionary position, doesn't make him a monk. Here are some of the most common sexual requests that he's building up the nerve to ask you right at this very minute:

1. He wants you to shave off your pubic hair: I'm sure at one point in your dating career, a guy has requested that you get a Brazilian wax. The first time a guy asked me to do this I was dumbfounded. Why in the world would a guy want a woman to look like a little girl? But then when the same request came up with another guy, I decided that either all men are pedophiles or they're all simply freaks. At the risk of having to put half of the population behind bars, I'll go with the freak thing on this one.

2. He wants to have anal sex: Vaginal intercourse seems to work pretty darn well. It's a design that's been perfected through millions of years of evolution and I think it's held up rather nicely. But men are natural explorers and want to look elsewhere in nature in search of satisfaction. And they seem to have found that place inside of your ass. It's mystifying how a man longs to put his favorite body part into a receptacle that's filled with crap. And once they've planted their flag in there, what other unexplored territory do they want to conquer next? Do they want to have nasal sex? Tear duct sex? Where does the madness end?

3. He wants you to try alternative sexual positions: When it comes to sex, men don't seem to be content with the standard positions. Instead they want to bend your limbs in ways that cut off your circulation. They want to arch your back so hard that it'll snap in two. And they want to contort your body into positions that could only be achieved had you been born boneless.

4. He wants to use props: Some men like to add spice to their sex life by integrating items that are raunchy, daring, and often, battery operated. Most of these items can vibrate, spin around, and stimulate body parts that you may not have know had the potential to be stimulated. Men are also fond of surprising you with things like handcuffs, whips, and a vast array of other equipment that is made out of leather.

5. He wants you to wear special outfits: You would think that just having a naked woman beside a guy would be stimulating enough. But oftentimes, men like to see their women dressed up in some kind of fantasy girl outfit. Some want them to wear lingerie that's so skimpy it looks like lacy dental floss. Others prefer them to be dressed as schoolgirls, nurses, or French maids. I never realized how easy Stevie Wonder's wife has it.

6. He wants to have a three-way: Show me a guy who doesn't fantasize about having a three-way and I'll show you one that's moved up to having a four-way. As far as I know, women don't have this fantasy. That's because there's really not much in it for us. We don't want to watch our man make love to another woman and we don't want to make love to another woman ourselves. But for some reason, the thought of two women in bed makes a guy's heart race faster than if it were driven by Mario Andretti.

7. He wants to have sex in public places: Some men need the additional stimulation of having sex with the risk of being caught. I'm sure that this strange behavior has something to do with their need for adventure, but their need doesn't seem to surpass my own need of not wanting to be seen naked in public. I have a hard enough time being seen naked in private, by myself.

There's a whole host of other kinky activities that men try to persuade women to participate in. Some want us to watch porn or to talk dirty during sex. Some try to lure us into doing special activities by giving them deceiving names like a pearl necklace. This way we think that we're getting a bauble when all we're really getting is screwed.

Bad Moves

Most men think that they're sexual dynamos. They pride themselves on being good lovers and knowing how to please a woman. Unfortunately, their knowledge of what women like in bed is as vast as their knowledge of knowing how to replace an empty roll of toilet paper.

Their first sexual faux pas is their lack of understanding of the female anatomy. Although most men are aware that a woman has a clitoris, very few know precisely where it is. It seems that the clitoris is the Bin Laden of female body parts. But instead of spending time learning all they can about its whereabouts, they simply grope you down there like a blind man in hopes of getting somewhere in the general proximity.

Another bad move that a man can make is the blowjob tug of war. This is when he puts his hand on your head and pushes it down while you struggle to push it back up. For you, a blowjob is a very personal and intimate activity. For him, it's seen more as an essential medical procedure to prevent blue balls and is as much of a necessity as sucking the venom from a snakebite.

"I once dated a guy who had a house filled with everything from sex tapes to strap-ons. He told me that he'd given a friend of his a tour of where he kept everything and made him swear to come over and get rid of it all if he died.**"**

—Deb

Men also have the annoying habit of being rough on your breasts. They get so aroused by these two big blobs of fat that they just can't seem to keep their hands off them. They twist them and pull them and kneed them like bread dough. Maybe subconsciously they're hoping that if they do, like the dough, they'll double in bulk.

Then there are those men who have the habit of making odd noises during sex. Sometimes they moan and groan so intensely that it sounds like they're eating crème brûlée while having sex. Sometimes their breathing becomes so labored, they can't get air in fast enough and they emit a whistling noise not unlike a boiling teapot. As you already know about me, I'm sensitive to certain noises. But strangely enough, I'm also sensitive to the lack of noise as well. If a guy is completely silent, I feel like a standup comedian doing my best act in front of a silent crowd.

There are plenty of other moves that men can perform that vary from odd to perverse. They like to suck on your toes. They like to lick your butt. But by far, the worst is a guy who likes to pee on you. Sure, he calls it a golden shower hoping that you'll like anything that has to do with precious metal, but I just don't get it. The way I see it, if you date a guy who associates sex with pee, urine for trouble.

Got Viagra?

One sure way to make the evening a downer is if he can't get it up. After working all your best moves and performing your most seductive tricks, your guy still lies there in neutral. Like all women, the first thing that you do is take it personally. Of course there must be something that you're doing wrong. You're not attractive enough. You're rubbing him the wrong way. Your butt looks too big in your G-string. So you kick things up a notch in hopes of proving yourself wrong. Like the good little multitasker that you are, you get your hands moving in one direction and your tongue moving in the other. You never imagined that the trick you learned as a kid when you patted your head and rubbed your belly would come in so handy as a grownup. But still, even with all your hard work, your guy is still as hard as Brie cheese.

Of course, the first thing that he says is that he's never had this problem before. And it could be that he's telling the truth. I've often heard that this condition happens to all guys at one time or another. But then again, maybe he isn't telling you the truth. Maybe he always had as hard a time getting it up as Howard Hughes did with the Spruce Goose. The fact is that impotence is the most common kind of erectile dysfunction and affects up to 30 million men in the United States alone. If you're like me and always choose the slowest checkout line at the supermarket, you have a huge chance of being with one of these men.

Although many times the cause of impotence is psychological, the reason for it could also be caused by a physical condition, and there's an easy way to tell the difference. All you need to do is to wake up before he does in the morning and look under the covers. If he's pitched a pup tent in his shorts, you know that the problem is all in his head. Luckily we live in an age of that little purple pill, which, just like a good bra, can give your man the lift and support that you both desperately need.

A Sex Drive That's Stuck in Neutral

When it comes to sexual desire, most people assume that men have a stronger libido than women. Men are seen as having veracious sexual appetites, ready to go at a moment's notice. Women, on the other hand, are thought of as having an appetite as small as Lara Flynn Boyle's.

But that's not always the case. I once dated a man who wasn't all that interested in sex. He rarely instigated it and when I did, he'd stop me and tell me how much better it would be if we waited. For some reason he seemed to confuse sex with fine wine that got better with age.

You may think it's odd that a strapping, healthy man could have such a low libido. I'll bet if this were to happen to you, the first thought that you'd have is that he must be gay. But it seems that a low libido is actually more common than you would imagine. One of the biggest reasons for it is stress. Men work longer hours and their commutes are far greater than they were a decade ago. As men are putting more time and energy into getting ahead, they seem to be a lot less concerned with getting head.

If you want to put some more heat in your man's oven, buy yourself a sexy lacy number with garters and stockings. Men just love that stuff. If that doesn't work, rent an adult video and hand him a stack of dirty magazines. If your partner's low libido is still giving you a headache, take two aspirins and call your doctor in the morning.

It's not that your doctor can do anything about it, but maybe *he'll* want to have sex with you.

The Beached Whale

The difference between the sexes isn't only restricted to innie and outtie body parts. It's also apparent when it comes to who will ask for directions and who will man the grill during a barbecue. And, there's also a very big difference when it comes to postsexual activity. After sharing our physical selves with another person, women long to feel a deep emotional connection with them as well. We want to cuddle and laugh, and have pillow talk for hours on end. But men aren't in agreement with this desire. The only thing they want to do after having sex is roll over and play dead. They don't want to cuddle or laugh or talk. When it comes to sex, men are like a judge's gavel and when they're done with their pounding, the court is adjourned.

During his twenty-minute state of semiconsciousness, you can choose to be upset or you can use this time to your advantage. While your beached whale is still resting on shore, you can finally do the one thing that you've been wanting to do since you started dating: Snoop! Admit it. You know you've been tempted. Before you get any more emotionally vested into this relationship, you want to discover any hidden secrets. So if you're at his place and he's lying there like dead weight, now's the time to do it.

Hidden Secrets

What to Look For	Where to Find It
Barely Legal magazine (*a magazine filled with girls who are barely eighteen*)	They are hidden under acceptable subscriptions or wedged between books in his bookshelf.
Porn videos	These are found where all his other videos are. If he has kids they can be harder to spot. Look for labels like "Work Graphics" or "Escrow Briefings."
Bank statements	Not only do you want to see his credit limit, but you also want to track his spending habits. You have the right to know if he was at the No-Tell Motel the night he told you his aunt Gertrude was in town.
Sex toys	When it comes to sex toys, the question isn't if he has them (I'd worry more if he didn't) but what kind they are. You may be able to stomach a vibrator or two, but when you find a rotating dildo or something called a butt plug, you may tend to worry. Sex toys are always conveniently located close to the bed.

If you don't have the nerve to snoop when he's right next to you, the very least you could do to take advantage of his condition is to ask him for something that you really want. During his beached whale state of mind, he's sure to promise you anything. But because he may not remember what he said, be sure to get it in writing, have a tape recorder handy, or even have a witness. Hey, maybe a three-way does have a benefit for women after all.

Other Ways to Burn 150 Calories

Sure, being in between boyfriends is bad for your emotional well-being, but it can also be bad for your waistline as well. It seems that having sex burns about 150 calories every half-hour. In order to stay at your physical best, try substituting the following activities for each missed romp in the hay:

1. A half-hour of doing laundry
2. An hour of watching television
3. Fifteen minutes of walking
4. Twenty-five minutes of hard housecleaning
5. Ten minutes of shoveling snow
6. Two hours of driving

chapter nine

special dating dilemmas

As if dating isn't hard enough on its own, sometimes life can throw even greater challenges into the mix. And even though many of these challenges are no fault of your own, it will be you who will have to pay the high price for them. Dating can be a tough road to hoe even when you are young and unencumbered, with a happy spirit and a flat stomach, but sometimes the road can become littered with so many potholes that it is hard not to veer off course.

There are dozens of possible reasons that pursuing a romance can become more of a challenge. Some of these challenges can be physical and others can be emotional. In either case, these experiences can leave your body weak and your energy drained. But thanks to time, support from friends and family, and prescription medication, you will find that you can once again be a part of the dating world.

Most of these dating hurdles are very commonplace today. Just a few decades ago, people only talked about these scenarios in hushed tones. But today they're as much a part of acceptable conversation as hemorrhoid cream and vaginal suppositories. Because they are so commonplace, help for these dating obstacles is as easy to find as, well, as hemorrhoid cream and vaginal suppositories. So if you find yourself suddenly challenged to get back into the dating game, be sure to keep your friends and family close, and that prescription medication even closer.

Dating After Divorce

Because I've never gone through a divorce, I had to rely solely on interviews with my girlfriends in order to write this segment. And I tell you, by doing so, I learned a lot about the sex life of a divorcée. Before I talked with them, I naively thought that a divorced woman would have a difficult time getting back in the dating saddle because of her incredible heartache. I would have thought that she'd need time to pamper herself, boost her self-esteem, and plan her strategy for taking that bastard for everything that he's worth before hopping back in the sack again. But it seems that I couldn't have been farther from the truth (except for the "taking that bastard" stuff), because plenty of newly divorced women are actually horny as hell.

The reason for this is simple and makes perfect sense. By the time that the marriage dies, the romance has died long before. When one of the two spouses finally gets the courage to say, "It's over," it has usually been months since the two of them have had sex. They were both too busy making war instead of love. They were too angry to sleep in the same bed, and too hurt to reach out to each other.

But even though a newly divorced woman is ready to take the plunge and start dating again, she may find that there isn't much water left in the pool. Because she's had so much experience when it comes to matters of the heart, she isn't happy starting at the bottom of the heap with all of the bottom feeders. She can't go back to putting up with men who don't call when they say they will and those who are forever in the bathroom when the check arrives. She's much too qualified to start back in the "dating mailroom" where all of the novices of love hang out. She wants more.

In addition to the frustration of finding a man who's worthy of her, she also has to relearn the rules of the dating playing field. Depending on when she last dated, there could be many things for her to figure out. For the past few years or even decades, she's spent most of her time dealing with one man. Therefore, she'll have to make many adjustments. The once-hip restaurants she used to go to have been turned into strip malls, and the music that she was once seduced by is now sold on TV as an oldie but goodie. Suddenly, a newly divorced woman doesn't quite fit into the dating world anymore, and she certainly doesn't fit into the dating clothing of today's world that's far too tight and much too low-cut.

The only silver lining on this black cloud is that there is a whole new breed of men that she can now consider dating that she adamantly rejected years before. That breed is that of divorced men. Before she was married, she was never much interested in going out with a divorced man because he usually came with too much baggage. He had an ex-wife and maybe even some kids. But now both she and the divorced man are in the same league. No longer does she see him as someone who's been tossed away. She now looks at him as someone that's grown up and matured and has learned a lot about what makes a good marriage work and the art of saying "Yes, dear." A divorced woman now sees that marriages are like pancakes and you should be able to throw the first one away.

So if you're now one of the millions of newly divorced women, I wish you well. I hope now that the papers are signed and the ink is dry, enough time has passed that your pain is lessened and your horniness has increased. I hope that you find a man who gives you exactly what your first husband made you realize that you need, so that the next time you get married, you can enjoy a pancake that's light and fluffy.

Dating After Your Heart's Been Broken

Man, oh man, if having your heart broken isn't one of life's most painful events, I don't know what is. Who among us hasn't walked down this rocky road that's paved with rusty nails and hot coals? If you have yet to experience this kind of agony, chances are it's only a matter of time until your heart will pull up to the station and fill up on this horrendous emotion.

Having a broken heart affects your day-to-day existence. You wake up in the morning in a happy, sleepy haze and then suddenly, like a bullet to the chest, the memory of the breakup returns. In an instant, you're overwhelmed with pain as you remember how the one person who you loved more than anyone else on this planet tossed you away like a pair of holey underwear. Somehow you manage to get your-self out of bed, scrape your heart off the floor along with last night's wads of tear-stained tissue, and summon up the strength to live life for one more day.

And what a painful day it is. Everything you do reminds you of him. You pour yourself a bowl of his favorite cereal, which you would buy just for him. You walk past the vacant spot in front of your building where he used to park when he stayed over. You can't drive down a street or go into a store without thinking of the time that you went there together. Your whole body is just one big ball of pain.

But that doesn't stop your friends from telling you that you should get back out there and start dating again. They try to convince you that when you fall off a horse, you have to get right back on it and keep on going. Me, I believe if you fall off a horse, you should lie in bed and watch daytime television until you've eaten your weight in Dove Bars. To me a broken heart is like any other organ that's gone through a massive trauma. You need to rest for a while so it has adequate time to heal. It needs to form a protective scab so it won't get hurt again too soon. How long will this process take? That depends on you. People heal at different rates and men seem to heal faster than any woman. The last time I was dumped, I was replaced in the time it took to make a three-minute egg.

You'll know your heart's had enough time to heal when you see a guy on the street who makes you salivate heavily. But tread lightly and act smart. Don't leave yourself open to more pain. Don't ask mutual friends how your ex is doing (you don't want to know). Don't drive by his place to see what he's up to (you don't want to see). You need to realize that if you find out anything at all upsetting, that scab will rip right off and you'll be back on your sofa eating Dove Bars again.

But don't get me wrong. I'm not advising that you plunge into a serious relationship right off the bat. During this emotional stage, your inner voice that you rely on to steer you in the right direction when it comes to men is driving drunk. Because of the breakup, that voice is so disoriented that she can no longer be trusted. You don't have the same power to accurately assess a guy and you can easily choose one that is wrong for you.

But that doesn't mean that you can't go out and date, and I bet that you'll learn a lot by doing so. In between the exhausting conversation about how many brothers and sisters some new guy has, you may find some clues as to what went wrong in your previous relationship. Because you don't have the same issues with this new man, you can see how you used to walk around on eggshells with your ex for fear of setting him off. You'll notice how little love he showed you and how much he took you for granted. Now that you have some distance and perspective, you can see that it was only a matter of time until your old relationship ended. And it wasn't until you went out with a new man that you were able to see things so clearly.

66 It's funny looking back at how heartsick I was when Brendon broke up with me. I thought my whole world was over and that I'd never get out of my depression. But now I'm so grateful to him for dumping me because if he hadn't, I would have never gotten engaged to Steve. I've gone from hating him to wanting to buy him a nice bottle of wine. **99**

—Susan

I know you may not believe me now, but I'll bet there'll come a day when you actually thank your ex for breaking up with you. You'll realize that he wasn't the one for you after all and if you two had stayed together, you would not have been happy. One day down the road you'll stop glorifying your old relationship and will come to realize that if your past relationship was meant to be, it would have been.

Dating As an Older Woman

Dating when you're past the age of forty and have never been married is becoming more common than ever. One reason is that women have found so much satisfaction in their careers that they don't need a man to satisfy them. They have demanding schedules and plenty of friends and coworkers to keep them busy. They don't need a man to keep them company or pay for them. The second biggie for an older population of single women is that they've simply never met a man they wanted to marry. Or if they did, the stupid idiot head never asked them to marry him. But no matter how you arrived on the more mature dating field, you can expect to need to rub Ben Gay on aches and pains that you didn't have to deal with when you were playing in a younger arena.

By far the biggest problem to deal with is the sparse selection of good men. When you were in your twenties and thirties, the pool of available men was about the size that you'd find at the Olympics. But now the water has evaporated down to the size of a kiddie pool. The reason for this is simple. By the time a man reaches forty, he is already married if he wants to be in a committed relationship. And if his marriage doesn't work out, a divorced man tends to gravitate toward a younger woman who can make him feel younger as well. To make things even worse, many younger women tend to gravitate toward older men because they provide them with the maturity, stability, and jewelry that they so desperately need. Because of all these factors, your chances of finding a man your age to play with are as slim as Martha Stewart developing a sweet disposition.

Because of this depressing fact, women over forty are forced to raise their age acceptance level of a man to that of one that's at least a decade older than they are. Sure there are some benefits, like if he has children, they'll be grown and out of the house. But there will be many more things that you'll need to get used to when dating a man who has a little snow on the roof:

- Many of his body parts can be taken off and put back on, like his teeth and hair. This may appeal to you if you liked playing with LEGOs as a kid.
- You'll still be able to be wined and dined as long as it's during the early-bird special.
- He'll grow more hair out of places like his ears, nose, and eyebrows. It's like dating one giant Chia Pet.
- He'll be far less malleable than a younger man who would bend over backwards to make you happy. An older man is more like a Gumby that's riddled with arthritis.
- His skin will hang looser from his body. Although this may not be very visually stimulating, you will have some places to hide small Christmas presents.
- If the two of you ever have kids, you can save some money and have them share the diapers and walker with your husband.

If you're one of those lucky women over forty who finds an incredible older man that still acts young and doesn't leave his left-hand turn signal on when he drives, consider yourself very lucky. If not, maybe you'll be lucky in another way and find that your vision will start to decline like most women your age so that you don't really see all of his imperfections.

Dating After the Death of a Spouse

When you're single because of a divorce, it can be a very frustrating situation. But when you're single because your husband has died, all you feel is despair. With no fault of your marriage and no say of your own, you're suddenly on your own. Sometimes, in an instant, you lose your partner, your lover, and your best friend, leaving you depressed, lonely, and deeply saddened.

Before you're even able to lift your head off the pillow, you have a mountain of hurdles to overcome. There's a funeral to plan for, medical bills to pay, insurance forms to fill out, and legal red tape to cut through. And of course, there are the many stages of grief that you'll have to travel through before you come out on the other side. The very last thing on your mind is fixing your hair so you can hit the club scene again. In fact, the whole idea of finding someone else to be with seems utterly absurd.

Dating after a death is the hardest kind of dating to deal with. Your marriage didn't end because there were problems. You weren't forced to stay together because of the kids. You have to come to terms with the fact that no amount of counseling will ever get the two of you back together and there is

> **❝** I've been single for twenty-two years now since my husband passed away. Whenever I heard there was an available man my age in the neighborhood, I'd try to meet him, but there were always a dozen other women with casseroles in line ahead of me. **❞**
>
> —My grandma

no chance of a reconciliation. It's just over and there's nothing at all that you can do to fix it.

But there might come a day when the thought of dating may not be so fleeting. It may stick in your brain long enough for you to actually decide that it's something that you're ready to do. Grief can be very isolating and the idea of going through another holiday alone may be more than you can bear.

So, maybe you accept a fix-up from a friend or you take a chance on your tax attorney whose been flirting with you. Somehow you gather the strength to get out there again. But don't expect smooth sailing in the sea of love. Usually there are many conflicted feelings that you'll have to face. Don't be surprised if you compare your date to your loved one or even feel like you're cheating.

If you're overwhelmed by a wave of emotions, head back to dry land and try again later. Maybe you need more time to grieve or maybe this dating thing brought back too many painful memories. If you know in advance that the sea will be rocky for a while, you won't think that there's anything wrong with you or that this is in any way your fault. You just may need to hold on a little longer. Whatever you feel is fine. However much time you take is fine. And if you decide that you want to find a new man to love, know that it's okay to keep your old love alive as well.

Dating with Low Self-Esteem

Sometimes the biggest obstacle of dating is one that we put on ourselves. We fully believe that because of some mental or physical trait, we're not worthy of finding love. Maybe we feel that no man could ever love us because we're not attractive enough or funny enough or have too much ambition or not enough sex appeal. When it comes to competing with other women in the dating world, there are many reasons why you'll think yourself an unworthy competitor.

I know that I've been a victim of low self-esteem myself. I remember during one of my lowest moments of self-loathing, I saw a documentary on TV about a pair of adult female conjoined twins who were attached at the forehead. One of the sisters was about half the size of a normal woman and she had to sit on a bar stool with wheels on it so that her sister could drag her along with her. When asked about their dating life, both sisters said they had boyfriends and that being conjoined twins didn't hinder their love life in any way. While I should have felt inspired by these women, I only felt sorry for myself. If a guy can be attracted to a woman who has a sister attached to her face, why couldn't I find one to love me despite a few pimples and a weak chin?

Feeling good about yourself doesn't have anything to do with how you look on the outside. My cousin Jessica is a prime example of this. She's the most beautiful creature I've ever seen in real life. She has flawless skin, a slender figure, and incredible bone structure, which is why she's graced the pages of many magazines. To this day I find myself staring at her trying to comprehend how we could share any of the same DNA. But does she have self-confidence and a high self-esteem? Not at all. She's forever criticizing one bodily feature or another because she thinks it falls short in some way. Her thighs are too big. Her breasts are too small. She's even lamented that her belly button doesn't go in far enough. Her belly button, for heaven's sake.

I know how easy it is to fall into a sea of self-loathing. I once had a physical condition that destroyed my self-confidence. When I was in high school, I found out that my spine had decided it didn't want to grow straight anymore and that the only way to straighten it out was to wear a full steel body brace for six years. As you can imagine, I was not pleased. There I was trying to fit in during my teen years, and I stuck out like a sore metallic thumb. I felt as ugly as anyone could feel and thought that my only redeeming quality was that I could get a magnet to stick to my blouse.

Strangely enough, looking back, I wouldn't change one thing about the experience. Sure, I wasn't too thrilled that I didn't have one date in all of those six years, and I wasn't too fond of the fact that if someone bumped into me, they could dislocate their shoulder. But going through that experience made me come out a lot stronger and not just because I had to carry around a fifteen-pound brace all day. I realized that my self-imposed lack of confidence was a far bigger crutch to my happiness than my brace could ever have been.

I'll bet that most of you are guilty of criticizing yourself like Roger Ebert does a new film. Whether it's a poor body image, lack of confidence, or a belly button that doesn't go in far enough, we all seem to find some reason to sabotage our love life. The funniest part about it is that we go through all of this self-loathing because we don't feel we're worthy of a certain guy. And have you taken a good look at the guy it is that you want? As I've already pointed out, most guys are far less attractive than we are, but do they seem to care? Do you see any of them obsessing about enlarged pores or hairy nipples? If you ask me, men should be worried that they're not good enough for us, not the other way around!

Dating After You Have Kids

You've all heard the expression that when you're pregnant, you're eating for two. Well, when you have kids, it seems that you're dating for two. That's because after you've gone forth and multiplied, you have to consider how your actions affect your offspring. You don't have the luxury of dating men the way you used to. You can't stay out until the wee hours of the morning. You can't have any one-night stands. And you can't go off on a romantic getaway for the weekend at the drop of a hat. Well, I guess you could, but your kids would be taken away by social services because you left them to fend for themselves while you were off tanning in the Keys.

When you have kids, you have to look for different traits in a man. You want to find someone who's going to be good to your children instead of someone who's just good in bed. You need someone who's financially stable instead of a free-loader. And it certainly doesn't hurt if he knows how to stop a tantrum in its tracks and can make a good grilled cheese sandwich. In addition, you may want to date a man who's outgrown the need to paint their chests with their team's colors before a big game . . . well, never mind, you'll be waiting forever for that one to happen.

Where you look for a man will probably differ as well. Options that are available to a non-mommy may not be in your best interests. For instance, an office romance may not be such a good move since your family is dependent on your weekly paycheck. Online dating may be too risky because you can't guarantee the quality of the men out in cyberspace. And a bar setting would be ridiculous since you'd probably never find a guy that could commit to you longer then it takes to drink his beer.

Another big challenge to dating when you have kids is finding the time to actually do so. Unlike women who never had the need of breast shields, you have diapers to change and science projects to supervise. You have bedtime books to read and teeth to brush. The key to finding time to date: be lucky enough to have joint custody. This way, you have the luxury of having a couple of nights a week free while knowing that your kids are well taken care of. Besides, sitters are expensive and can take a big bite out of your alimony checks. If you don't have an ex or have one that's not a part of your children's lives, you have an even tougher time of things. If this is your case, don't expect to date until you bring someone to your child's wedding.

Anyone who's tried to find a man when they have kids knows the script all too well. When you finally meet a guy who looks nice, seems descent, and doesn't look familiar from any newspaper headline, it's only a matter of time before he asks the inevitable question, "So, do you have any kids?" It's at this point that you've reached a fork in the road of romance. It's a salad fork actually, because once you tell him that you do, there are three possible tongs. One is for him to say, "Really? So do I!" A second is that he'll appear open to the idea and ask for more details like how many kids you have and how old they are. And the third possible tong is for him to excuse himself for a minute and sneak out the window in the men's room. This, my friend, is by far the most common tong.

If you are fortunate enough to find a decent guy to date, you have the dilemma of deciding when to introduce him to your kids. Some women don't waste any time and introduce them right from the start. Others wait until they have a ring on their finger to avoid getting their kids attached to a man who may not go the distance. Me, I'd advise that you err on the side of caution on this one. Kids whose parents are divorced have been through enough mental anguish. They're forced to choose sides, they have to shuffle from home to home, and they have to come to terms with the fact that they'll never get mommy and daddy back together. Any further pain that you can spare them may just save you a fortune in future therapy bills.

As you can see, once you create a little tax deduction, you also create difficulties finding love. But just like you are open to dating divorcés now that you're divorced, you are now open to dating another new kind of man as well. Before you had kids, you may not have been interested in pursuing a relationship with a man that did. You saw his kids as freckle-faced pieces of baggage that seemed too heavy a burden to carry. But now that you have your own set of matching luggage, you realize that it isn't a burden at all. In fact, it's an advantage. Men who are fathers understand the difficulties and limitations that you face when you have kids. They understand when you cancel plans at the last minute because the sitter never showed or Jr. wanted to see what would happen if he stuck a pea up his nose. They know too well how tired you can be at the end of the day and that you can never get the Barney theme song out of your head no matter how hard you try.

So if you are trying to date while juggling a family without a father, be patient. Wait until you find a man who's in it for the long run and take your time introducing him to your kids. If you play your cards right, you can all become one happy family and sing that annoying little theme song together.

Things to Remember When You Date After You Have Kids

If you're a newcomer to dating after you've had kids, there are some simple guidelines to follow. Sure they seem easy, but you'll be surprised how hard they can be to follow. Old habits can be quite hard to break.

- Don't ask the waitress for crayons.
- Avoid constantly asking your date if he needs to go potty.
- Don't cut up his meat for him.
- If he swears, don't give him a time out.
- Avoid referring to yourself in the third person, like "Mommy will get that for you"—unless, of course, he asks you to.
- Don't blow his nose for him.
- Don't tell him he can't have dessert if he didn't finish his meal.
- If he gets food on his mouth, don't lick your thumb and wipe it off.

chapter ten

you did it!

Congratulations! Success is yours! You were like a salmon swimming upstream. You persevered through strong currents and incredible obstacles and miraculously found a great guy who you like and who likes you in return. You can say whatever you want without feeling like you're going to scare him away. You know that the two of you will spend the weekend together even though neither of you have bothered to ask. You know that he likes garlic on his pizza, the name of the quarterback on his favorite football team, and that he gets turned on when you call him "babe." You crossed the bridge of relationships and, dare I say it, you made it to the other side. Congratulations! You now have yourself a boyfriend!

Now that the end of the tumultuous first few months is over, your relationship is settling into something that's more solid and comfortable. You don't feel the pressure to fill every moment with conversation and he's seen you without your makeup and still tells you that you're cute. You've confessed some secrets to him, like you love to eat pickled watermelon rinds with ice cream and that you've named

your car Nina. By now you've had that talk about not dating anyone else and have felt the sheer bliss of hearing him
tell you that he loves you. You never thought that you'd
get here. You were convinced that love was like that rebate
check you were promised when you bought your laptop that
never seemed to make it to your door. But it did finally come
and you are truly happy.

I'm not saying that this relationship is guaranteed to
go the distance. You may never celebrate your silver anniversary or, for that matter, even make it to your high school
reunion next fall, but you've made it this far and that's a
cause to celebrate.

Love works in mysterious ways and you realize that all
those years of searching for it is well worth the price. All
those pitiful blind dates that you went on, those office flirtations that went nowhere, and those painful unreciprocated
crushes were instantly forgotten the first time you heard
your guy introduce you as his girlfriend.

Now that you're a part of a couple, you find that your
friends and family treat you differently. You're seen as more
grown-up and respected, and feel like you've been given the
key to an exclusive club. Maybe it's because the pity and frustration they felt for you no longer exist. Now they can ask
you other questions besides, "So, are you seeing anyone?"

Sure, you may be nervous. It's scary to give your tender
and delicate heart to someone who has the power to stomp on
it like wine grapes. But facing a future where the most exciting thing in your week is the arrival of the latest *TV Guide*
is just as scary. So enjoy. After all your hard work, you know
you have someone to share your life with. Someone who cares
about you and who has your best interest at heart. Someone
to kiss on New Year's Eve and to remind you which side of

your car the gas tank is on. Someone to take you to the airport and to offer a helping hand whenever you have a stubborn jar that doesn't want to open. Now you have a shoulder to cry on and a hand to hold, and most of all, now you have someone to love! So smile big and revel in the moment. These truly are the best of days and make for the sweetest memories that you'll have in life. I wish you all the best!

Ten Signs That You Have a Boyfriend

1. You've made up those cute yet embarrassing pet names for one another.
2. He's met your family and likes you anyway.
3. You can sleep together without feeling like you have to have sex.
4. You've farted in front of him.
5. He knows when you're expecting to have PMS so that he can walk around wearing a hardhat.
6. You can put your zit cream on before you go to bed again.
7. You've gone away together and still like one another.
8. You don't have to wrap your tampon tubes in toilet paper before throwing them in the wastebasket.
9. You've pooped while he's been over.
10. You're happy!

appendix

single-girl resources

Good Movies to Rent
to Make You Believe in Love

When Harry Met Sally: Meg Ryan, Billy Crystal

American President: Michael Douglas, Annette Bening

Shrek: Mike Myers, Eddie Murphy, Cameron Diaz

Ever After: A Cinderella Story: Drew Barrymore

Pretty Woman: Julia Roberts, Richard Gere

The Princess Bride: Cary Elwes, Robin Wright Penn

Breakfast at Tiffany's: Audrey Hepburn, George Peppard

Gone with the Wind: Vivien Leigh, Clark Gable

Beauty and the Beast: Paige O'Hara, Robby Benson

Annie Hall **(yes, I know it ends on a downer, but you'll laugh so hard you won't even care):** Diane Keaton, Woody Allen

Good Movies to Rent
When You Have a Specific Problem with Finding Love

Feeling heavy?
See any movie that stars Marilyn Monroe, who would be considered obese by today's standards.

Recently stood up?
Watch *Deliverance, Cold Mountain, Midnight Express,* or any other movie where men suffer.

Your date's not as attractive as you'd like?
Rent *The Full Monty* and you can see how adorable a man can be even though he may not be that good-looking.

Feeling sorry for yourself that you're not married?
Watch *Sleeping with the Enemy, Enough,* or *The Color Purple* and revel in your singleness.

Tired of dating men who don't treat you right?
Watch *Forrest Gump* and realize how sweet a nice guy can be.

Disgusted with all men?
Get *Personal Best, "Better than Chocolate,"* or any movie that stars Ellen DeGeneres.

Things to Do That May Be Much
More Satisfying Than Going on a Date

- Get your car detailed.
- Take a belly-dancing class.
- Volunteer to read to kids at your local library.
- Learn how to make sushi.
- Walk down your street and fill up the expired meters before the cars get tickets.
- Have your eyebrows professionally done.
- Splurge and buy a small tin of caviar for dinner.
- Have some friends over for a wine-tasting party (or a frost your own cupcake party . . . whatever your sin of choice may be).
- Try one of those spray-tanning services.
- Buy fresh flowers for your home or plant ones in your garden.

Great Places for a Single Girl
to Travel to By Herself

New York: You can shop in the best stores in the world and don't have to feel guilty trying on clothes knowing that he's bored to tears.

Hershey, Pennsylvania: You can indulge in chocolate without having someone watch in amazement at how much you can put away.

New Orleans: Not only can you "laissez les bons temps rouler" (let the good times roll), but you can eat a bowlful of delicious red beans and rice and not have to hold in your farts.

Anyplace that doesn't have a golf course: You don't have to spend your whole vacation thinking that the man you're with would rather be there than with you.

Anyplace that doesn't have a hunting season: You don't have to end your vacation by pretreating blood stains on his clothes.

A spa: You get all the benefits of being rubbed and pampered without dealing with anyone else's needs.

Alaska: Sure, it has breathtaking scenery, but it also has the highest ratio of single men to single women than any place in the country.

Great Books for a Single Girl to Read

Diana: The Portrait, **by Rosalind Coward:** Put to rest the idealized notion that once we meet our prince, we'll live happily ever after.

The Proper Care and Feeding of Husbands, **by Dr. Laura Schlessinger:** Get a glimpse of some of the problems and hassles of having a husband so you can better realize that the grass isn't necessarily so much greener on the other side.

The Da Vinci Code, **by Dan Brown:** It won't really help you learn anything about love, but it's one heck of a good read and there isn't even one kissing scene to make you feel self-pity.

My Life, **by Bill Clinton:** You can just skip over the political stuff and cut right to his affair with Monica and realize that even the most charismatic, powerful leader of our time is flawed. Hopefully it'll open your eyes to the fact that there is no such thing as the "perfect" man.

44 Uses for a Dog and 41 Uses for a Cat, **by Harriet Ziefert:** Discover the various ways that your beloved pet can do things for you around the house, making the void of not having a man so much less.

Complete Home How-To, **by Albert Jackson:** Sure, not having a man in your life may mean less sex, but it doesn't have to mean more household troubles. Learn how to repair your own broken garbage disposal and leaky toilet so that you don't have to be the helpless heroine.

Big Book of Knitting, **by Katharina Buss:** Face it. You have more time on your hands when you're not dating, so it's best to put them to good use. Not only can you make the best of the situation but you can also make a lot of great sweaters.

Great Revenge Tactics for a Single Girl
Who's Been Done Wrong by a Man

- Put a stinky wedge of cheese underneath his car hood. He won't notice it at first, but just a few miles down the road, he'll smell something as disgusting as himself.
- Write his name down on a piece of paper and put the paper inside the freezer. The theory behind this is that it will prevent him from moving on in life.
- Hide a Swiss Army knife inside of a small pocket in his luggage. This will cause a big security delay on his next romantic weekend trip.
- Smear Ben Gay on his deodorant. Now that you've been burned, it's only fair that his pits burn as well.
- Sign him up on a gay porn Web site. He'll spend eternity trying to stop all of his newfound e-mail.
- Order a popular catalog for him in the name of Mr. Dick Miniscule. Many stores are owned by a single parent company, so your ex will receive oodles of other mail under that name.

Best Ways to Get Rid of That Predate Zit

- If your big date is days away, be sure to clean your face thoroughly with an oil-free, fragrance-free cleanser that's PH balanced.
- If you have oily skin, use one that contains benzoyl peroxide or salicylic acid. Remember, don't scrub!
- Use a concealer that's the same shade as your skin. Blend it thoroughly. If your zit is a whopper, you may need to apply two coats.
- If your pimple is past the point of concealing, try applying an over-the-counter cortisone cream, Preparation H, or Vasocon-A eye drops.
- If you have the time and money, visit a dermatologist for a cortisone injection, which should make your pimple disappear. If only you could use the shot on yourself if your date turns out to be a total loser!

"Best" Necessities of a Single Girl

Best Chocolate: K Chocolatier, from Diane Krön. A favorite of Jacqueline Kennedy, Katharine Hepburn, and Barbra Streisand. Try the K Sensual for women only, "A box of seven experiences." Visit *www.dkron.com* or call (310) 248-2626.

Best shopping magazine: Lucky magazine. It follows fashion trends from city to city, shows what the stores are selling, and includes phone numbers on how to order the clothes that you'll see. To check it out, visit *www.luckymag.com.*

Best vibrator: The Rabbit Pearl. This is the vibrator that Charlotte was addicted to in *Sex and the City.* They called it "The Bunny" because it's so darn cute. To order call (888) LOVEINME.

Best raw cookie dough: Mr. Field's cookie dough. It is found in the freezer section of most supermarkets.

Best classic single girl novel: *Bridget Jones's Diary.* This book is available on *www.amazon.com.*

Best bubble bath: Lollia. This is according to Oprah, and if anyone knows about a good bubble bath, it's Oprah. It comes in both "Relax" and "Breathe." To order, visit *www. lollialife.com* or call (888) 8LOLLIA.

Best scented candle: Diptyque. They are available in forty-five different scents. To check them out and to order, visit *www.illumecandles.com.*

Best long-distance carrier: Working Assets. Not only do they donate 1 percent of their total revenue to over fifty nonprofit organizations, but they also send you a coupon every month for a pint of Ben & Jerry's ice cream for a whole year! To sign up go to *www.workingassets.com* or call (866) 753-6123.

Songs You Can Listen to
When You're in Love

"Love Me Tender," by Elvis Presley

"Wind Beneath My Wings," by Bette Midler

"When a Man Loves a Woman," by Percy Sledge

"Your Song," by Elton John

"Because You Loved Me," by Céline Dion

"I Think I Love You," by The Partridge Family

Whatever song the two of you chose to be your song

Songs to Avoid When You're Going Through a Heartbreak

"Alone Again, Naturally," by Gilbert O'Sullivan

"Without You," by Harry Nilsson

"One Is the Loneliest Number," by The Beatles

"I Fall to Pieces," by Patsy Cline

"I Can't Make You Love Me," by Bonnie Raitt

"How Am I Supposed to Live Without You," by Michael Bolton

Whatever song the two of you chose to be your song

Best Music to Listen to When
You're Going Through a Heartbreak

"I Will Survive," by Gloria Gaynor

"More Wine Waiter Please," by The Poor

"The Rose," by Bette Midler

"One Last Cry," by Brian McKnight

"Margaritaville," by Jimmy Buffett

Some of the Best Recipes to
Make the Most Popular Girly Drinks

This will be helpful whenever you want to celebrate being alone, toast to a new relationship, or get over a bad breakup.

Cosmopolitan: Combine 4 parts Citron Vodka, 2 parts Cointreau or triple sec, 1 part lime juice, and 2 parts cranberry juice in a martini shaker and pour into an iced martini glass.

Margarita: Rub the rim of a chilled glass with a lemon or lime wedge and then dip the glass in salt. Fill a shaker halfway with ice and mix with 1½ ounces of tequila, ¾ ounce of Cointreau or triple sec, and a splash of lime juice. You can also combine all ingredients in a blender if you like your margaritas blended.

Strawberry Daiquiri: Combine 1 scoop of ice, 1½ ounces of rum, a splash of sour mix, and ¼ cup of strawberries in a blender. Pour into a glass and add one of those adorable tiny umbrellas.

Apple Martini: Combine 1 part vodka and 1 part apple liquor in an iced martini glass. I've also found that substituting liquor for apple watermelon liquor makes a mighty fine drink as well!

Rum and Diet Coke: This one is pretty much a no-brainer. If you can't figure out the recipe for this, my guess is that you've already had enough to drink.

The Best Way to Get Rid
of Dating-Related Stains

Coffee (to help you wake up after tossing and turning all night anticipating the date): Rinse the back of the stain with cold water. Apply an enzyme detergent (like Tide, Cheer, or most major brands) and let soak for several minutes. Wash with an enzyme detergent.

Diet Coke (your drink at lunch with the girls while discussing your date that night): Blot the stain as soon as possible. Sponge or soak the stain in cold water. Rub with liquid enzyme detergent and let stand for several minutes. Launder in the hottest water that's safe for the fabric.

Chocolate (what you nibble on all day to calm your nerves before the date): Use a dull knife and scrape off as much as possible. Rinse the back of the stain with cold water. Apply an enzyme detergent and let soak in cold water from thirty minutes to several hours. Occasionally rub the stain with your fingers as it soaks.

Red wine stain (what you order on your date to help calm you down): Pour white wine, club soda, or water on the stain as soon as possible. Blot with an absorbent cloth and pour salt on the stain. Let it sit for two minutes. Rinse in cold water and then rub out the stain.

Semen (for when the date doesn't go as bad as you had expected): Hold the stain under cold, running water to help flush out the stain. Soak and agitate the fabric until loosened. If the stain remains, rub liquid laundry detergent into the stain and let set for several minutes. Wash the garment according to the label's instructions.

**Cheapest Places to Buy a House in the United States So
That You Can Afford One Without the Help of a Man***
(Except Maybe Your Dad, Who You May Need to Cosign the Loan)

Minot, North Dakota

Great Falls, Montana

Arlington, Texas

Billings, Montana

Killeen, Texas

*According to CNN on October 4, 2004

**The Places Where You're Least Likely to Be Able
to Afford a House on Your Single-Girl Income***

Lo Jolla, California

Beverly Hills, California

Santa Barbara, California

Palo Alto, California

Greenwich, Connecticut

*According to CNN on October 4, 2004

Best TV Channels for You to Watch
When You Don't Have a Man to Ridicule You

The Hallmark Channel: They play old, sappy shows that are great if you're in the mood for a good cry.

VH1: They make fun, hip programs.

SoapNet: They rerun that day's soaps at night that you missed while at work. On weekends they rerun the whole week's worth!

WE: It stands for "Women's Entertainment," and it's chock-full of movies that appeal to all of us with a uterus.

Oxygen: My favorite show is *Oprah After the Show*; at times, it can be more entertaining than the show itself.

TBS: They air the best chick flicks that you've no doubt seen a dozen times already but can't seem to get enough of.

The Food Network: My favorite shows include *30 Minute Meals with Rachael Ray* for good easy recipes, anything with Tyler Florence because he's so darn cute, and *Barefoot Contessa,* who lives in a gorgeous house in the Hamptons. You'll enjoy it for her cutting garden alone.

about the author

Joanne Kimes is the coauthor of the bestsellers *Pregnancy Sucks* and *Pregnancy Sucks for Men*. She has written for a number of children's and comedy television shows and has more than two decades of dating under her belt.

Printed in the United States
By Bookmasters